RESTROOMS

Housetraining

2nd Edition

September Morn

Howell
Book House™

Howell Book House

Published by Wiley Publishing, Inc., Hoboken, New Jersey

For general information on our other products and services or to obtain technical support please contact our Customer Care Department within the U.S. at (800) 762-2974, outside the U.S. at (317) 572-3993 or fax (317) 572-4002.

Wiley also publishes its books in a variety of electronic formats. Some content that appears in print may not be available in electronic books. For more information about Wiley products, please visit our web site at www.wiley.com.

Library of Congress Cataloging-in-Publication Data:

Morn, September B.
    Housetraining / September Morn.— 2nd ed.
        p. cm.—(Your happy healthy pet)
    ISBN-13: 978-0-7645-9918-7 (cloth : alk. paper)
    ISBN-10: 0-7645-9918-6 (cloth : alk paper)
    Dogs—Training. 2. Puppies—Training. I. Title. II. Series.
    SF431.M824 2006
636.7'0887—dc22
            2005017379

Printed in the United States of America

10 9 8 7 6 5 4 3 2 1

2nd Edition

Edited by Beth Adelman   Book design by Melissa Auciello-Brogan
Photo research by Marcella Durand   Cover design by Michael J. Freeland
Book production by Wiley Publishing, Inc. Composition Services

About the Author

September Morn has trained dogs professionally for more than thirty years, helping to integrate dogs into their owners' lives and homes, teaching both dogs and owners the skills they need to coexist happily. September teaches group classes and private lessons and conducts behavior seminars and training workshops. She also offers both in-home and distance consultations, helping people understand and change their dogs' behavior. September has aided humane shelters in setting up training programs to improve dogs' behavior and adoptability. To date, September has written more than 150 articles and 6 training books. She holds a BA in psychology, with a concentration in cognition and perception, from Western Washington University. September lives with several beloved dogs on her hobby farm in Washington State.

About Howell Book House

Since 1961, Howell Book House has been America's premier publisher of pet books. We're dedicated to companion animals and the people who love them, and our books reflect that commitment. Our stable of authors—training experts, veterinarians, breeders, and other authorities—is second to none. And we've won more Maxwell Awards from the Dog Writers Association of America than any other publisher.

As we head toward the half-century mark, we're more committed than ever to providing new and innovative books, along with the classics our readers have grown to love. This year, we're launching several exciting new initiatives, including redesigning the Howell Book House logo and revamping our biggest pet series, Your Happy Healthy Pet™, with bold new covers and updated content. From bringing home a new puppy to competing in advanced equestrian events, Howell has the titles that keep animal lovers coming back again and again.

Contents

Shopping List

Before you bring home your pup, stock up on the basic supplies you'll need. Here is a list of items you'll want to have on hand when your puppy arrives and in the days that follow.

- [ ] Food dish
- [ ] Water dish
- [ ] Dog food
- [ ] Leash
- [ ] Collar
- [ ] Crate
- [ ] Crate pad or blanket
- [ ] Portable exercise pen
- [ ] Hollow rubber chew toy (to stuff with food)

- [ ] Soft cuddle toy
- [ ] Training treats
- [ ] Training book
- [ ] Extra paper towels
- [ ] Enzyme-based cleaner
- [ ] Grooming brush and comb
- [ ] Nail trimming tool
- [ ] ID tag

This is your very special puppy, so you may want to buy some special items you've been thinking about. Use these spaces to jot them down so you won't forget them when you're on your shopping trip.

- [ ] _____
- [ ] _____
- [ ] _____
- [ ] _____
- [ ] _____
- [ ] _____
- [ ] _____
- [ ] _____
- [ ] _____

Pet Sitter's Guide

We can be reached at (___)_____-_____ Cellphone (___)_____-_____

We will return on _____ (date) at _____ (approximate time)

Dog's Name _____

Breed, Age, and Sex _____

Important Names and Numbers

Vet's Name _____ Phone (___)_____- _____

Address_____

Emergency Vet's Name _____ Phone (___)_____- _____

Address_____

Poison Control _____ (or call vet first)

Other individual to contact in case of emergency _____

_____

Care Instructions

Keep fresh water available at all times. The water bowl is (where) _____

_____

Feeding times, amounts, and special instructions: _____

_____

Feed the dog in this location: _____

Dog's approved elimination area is (where) _____

Take dog to eliminate at these times (or use chart in chapter 9): _____

_____

Exercise the dog this way (how and when) _____

When alone, the dog is to be confined (where) _____

Areas in house or yard where the dog is not allowed unattended _____

Where the dog sleeps _____

Grooming instructions _____

Medications or special care instructions _____

Other special care instructions _____

My dog's favorite playtime activities, quirks, and other tips _____

_____

Part I
About Housetraining

The Puppy

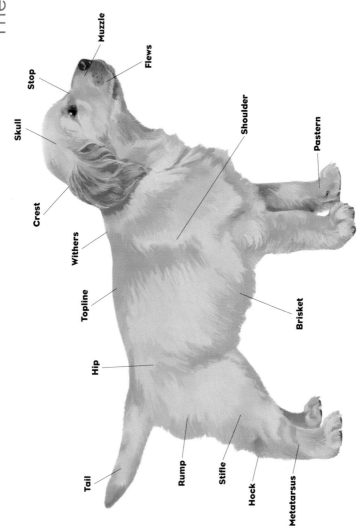

Muzzle

Flews

Stop

Skull

Shoulder

Crest

Pastern

Withers

Topline

Brisket

Hip

Tail

Rump

Stifle

Hock

Metatarsus

Chapter 1

Canine Cleanliness

Six little puppies squirm and wiggle, crawling closer to their mother's warmth and sweet milk. The litter is three days old. The pups can neither see nor hear at this age, and their eyes and ears won't open for about another week. Their sense of touch is working well though, as is their sense of smell. The puppies' pudgy little noses lead them to their mama, who is lying, full and fat with her abundant milk, ready to nurse them.

Six puppies nurse in a contented row at their dam's belly, making suckling noises and grunts of satisfaction. The mama dog pants softly as she watches her brood. The largest pup releases his suction hold and furiously nuzzles around, looking for a fuller spot at mama's milk bar. The pup tumbles over two nursing littermates then finds an unoccupied position and begins to nurse again, kneading his dam's belly with tiny round paws. Once again, all is right in the pup's world.

The dam's ears twitch toward a slightly different sound. The big pup is still nursing, but his snuffling, suckling sounds have changed. Now he's making a slightly different puppy grunt. Mama's nose goes to the pup immediately. She nuzzles her baby, then gently begins to lick his little belly and backside.

The pup wiggles, feeling his mother's attention, then becomes still for a moment. The stimulation of his dam's insistent lapping releases the pup's urine and feces. The mother's licking is vital to the pup's survival, for without this type of attention new pups are not able to eliminate their own body wastes.

The mama dog cleans away her pup's waste as he produces it, then she washes the pup from head to toe, removing every trace of odor. She repeats this with each pup in turn until all have relieved themselves and been cleaned. The dam tidies her whelping nest until it once again is spotless. Then she relaxes and naps for a short while with her clean, contented brood.

Early Puppy Development

Puppies sleep about 90 percent of their first two weeks of life, waking only to nurse and be cleaned. Their dark and quiet world is informed through their senses of smell and touch. Unable to control their own body temperature, the pups spend most of their time huddled together or cuddled against their dam.

By about eighteen days old, the pups have developed enough physical coordination and strength to progress from a belly crawl to a shaky walk. One of the first journeys a puppy takes is a few steps away from the sleeping corner to eliminate. Even very young pups seem to instinctively know that it's improper to soil their sleeping and eating quarters.

By three weeks of age, the pups have gained some control over their own elimination. They no longer require the stimulation of their mother's insistent licking. They can "go" on their own, although mama still nurses them and cleans up their body waste.

At first, the mother stays with her puppies around the clock, leaving them only when she must eat or relieve herself. As the pups grow, they become mobile and curious and start to follow mama when she leaves the whelping nest. When the mama dog stops a few steps away from the clean sleeping area, the pups, toddling close behind her, stop too. If they try to nurse, mama won't allow it right now. The pups mill around in frustration, then nature calls and they all urinate and defecate here, away from their bed. The dam returns to the nest with her litter waddling behind her. The puppies' first housetraining lesson has been a success.

Now about five weeks old, the pups are mobile and active, though still a bit clumsy. They begin to play games of stalking and pouncing on one another and their dam. Their eyesight and hearing are good now, and the sound of one puppy nursing brings all the others scrambling to dinner.

The pups have teeth now, and they're quite sharp. Their jaw muscles are growing stronger too, and when pups nurse too vigorously, those pinlike teeth hurt their mama's sensitive teats. She realizes it's time to start weaning her litter.

The Breeder's Job

When the pups are about 4 to 5 weeks old, they are growing too fast to be satisfied with mother's milk. The breeder begins to supplement their diet with a meat-and-cereal-based gruel or commercial puppy kibble soaked in water or milk.

Even when the puppies are eating solids, their dam still nurses them several times a day. Her milk supply is decreasing, though, and the pups are growing

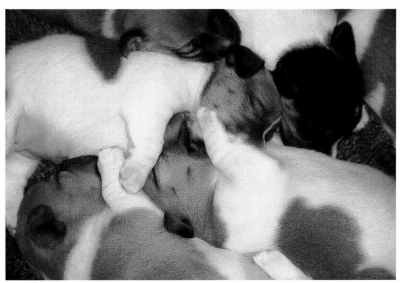

The mother dog must do almost everything for her new babies, including helping them to eliminate.

bigger and hungrier. Mama usually leaves the den area immediately after she suckles her pups. The breeder has securely placed a board across the entrance to the puppy corner. Mama can easily hop over this barrier, but it's too high for the pups to follow her.

They run after their dam as she leaves, hoping for just a bit more of her sweet milk, but she disappears over the barrier board. The pups mill around in frustration for a moment, then feel urgency in their bladders and bowels. The whole litter eliminates together. The pups then return to their sleeping corner to play for a few minutes before they all settle down for an after-dinner nap.

Once puppies begin eating solid foods, their dam no longer laps up their body wastes. The pups still need their mother to teach them important rules and customs of dog society, but the breeder now must take over their feeding and hygiene.

The breeder keeps the puppies clean and their living area sanitary by frequent and thorough housekeeping. Having planned far ahead for this birth, the breeder has saved the daily newspaper for several months and has asked friends to save theirs for him as well. He opens sections of the clean newspaper and spreads them thickly wall to wall in the pups' corner to absorb puppy piddles and water spills.

The breeder watches as the puppies eliminate, then deftly removes the soiled papers and replaces them with clean papers before they can traipse back through their messes. He has wisely arranged the puppy space so their bed, food, and drinking water are as far away from the gate as possible. This way, when the pups follow their mama as she leaves after nursing them, they will move away from their sleeping and eating area before eliminating. This helps strengthen the natural canine habit of keeping the inner den clean of body waste. Once formed, this habit will help the pups be readily housetrained when they are adopted into their permanent homes.

Potty Outdoors

As the puppies grow bigger and more energetic, the breeder begins to allow them to go outside for short periods in mild weather. One pup feels nature's call and walks to the edge of the play area to urinate. Several other pups notice and follow, realizing they also need to urinate. They stop near the spot where the first pup eliminated and use it too.

These puppies are accustomed to a clean den because their living space has been kept sanitary and relatively odor free, first by their dam and then by the breeder. The lack of odor and mess teaches the pups not to soil their sleeping and eating areas. They learn to move as far away as they can from the nest before squatting to eliminate. Soon these pups will go to their permanent homes, where proud owners will be delighted with how quickly the pups learn to follow the household cleanliness rules.

When you take your puppy, you will have to take on many of his mother's teaching duties.

Your Job

The day arrives for the puppy buyer to bring her new family member home. She is excited as she prepares to drive to the breeder's facility. She remembers to bring the chew toy she bought at the pet supply store yesterday, along with the other items her new pup will need.

The buyer loads a puppy-size crate into the front seat and buckles the seat belt securely around it. In the crate is a folded towel for bedding and absorbency, and she has brought more towels along just in case. She checks the map and the directions the breeder sent, then makes certain she has some bottled water for the pup.

Everything's ready to go. Well, almost—at the last minute she returns to the kitchen to grab spray cleaner, a roll of paper towels, and a big plastic trash bag for the inevitable spills, leaks, puppy piddles, and car sickness.

Getting the New Pup

As the buyer turns in to the breeder's driveway, an adult dog barks and the breeder opens his front door and waves. Two puppies snoozing in the shade in a clean, grassy pen awaken and run to the fence to see who has arrived.

The puppies place their little paws up on the fence and lick the buyer's fingers through the wire mesh. The pup reserved for the buyer is wearing a green nylon collar; the other puppy's collar is red. The green-collared puppy suddenly stops licking and gets down from the fence, walks a few steps away, sniffs, and urinates. The buyer notices the puppies' pen is very clean; she sees only one poop—right next to where the pup just eliminated.

After a flurry of final details, the new owner is ready to leave for home with her furry family member. The breeder has given her a sheaf of papers, including registration paperwork, immunization information, and instructions for feeding and care. He also sends along a week's supply of the food the pup is accustomed to eating.

The breeder nods in approval when he notices the new owner has brought a crate to safely transport the pup home. She loads the pup into the crate and checks the seat belt to be sure it's fastened securely.

The Trip Home

The puppy settles down in the crate, happily chewing on the toy his new owner brought for him. For the first few miles the pup occasionally gets restless, stops chewing his new toy, and whines. After he gets used to the movement and sound of the car, he settles back down and naps for about half an hour. When he wakes he starts to whine again, and the new owner realizes the pup probably needs a potty

Marking a Potty Spot for Your New Dog

While you're at the breeder's home (or the shelter, if that's where you will get your new dog), take a paper towel and blot up some urine from your pup or his littermates. Put this into a plastic bag and take it home. Place the soiled paper towel on the ground in the area where you'll be taking your pup to eliminate. Pour about half a cup of lukewarm water through the towel onto the ground to scent the new potty area with puppy urine, then dispose of the paper towel. The scent will give your pup the clue he needs to understand where he's supposed to eliminate at his new home.

break. She pulls into a rest stop and clips a lightweight leash to the pup's collar because it would be too dangerous to walk him off-leash here, so close to traffic.

The owner carries her pup to a likely spot and sets him on the ground. The puppy sits for a moment and scratches at the unfamiliar new collar, then gets up, sniffs the ground, turns half a circle, and urinates. Success! The owner waits a few minutes more, just in case the pup isn't finished. Sure enough, he goes again. Then they hit the road. The car's movement lulls the pup and he soon falls asleep in his crate again and doesn't wake up until they pull into the driveway at home.

At Home

The owner marks a potty spot in her backyard by pouring some water through the paper towel she'd soaked with urine from the pup's former home (see the box on this page). Then she takes the puppy out of his crate and carries him to the marked spot so he can relieve himself. Success—times two! Afterward, she brings the puppy into the kitchen, where she has already set up a portable folding exercise pen as a puppy corral with several layers of newspaper covering the floor.

As she prepares supper, she allows the pup to play around her feet where she can keep an eye on him in case he acts restless, like he might need to eliminate. When she feeds the pup, she places his dinner bowl in the far corner of the pen, next to his crate/bed and tip-proof water bowl.

After the pup finishes eating, the owner takes him out to the potty area, where he immediately relieves himself. The owner praises the puppy and gives herself a mental pat on the back for preparing everything she needed ahead of time. She begins to realize that because of the pup's good cleanliness start at his breeder's home, plus her own preparedness, housetraining might turn out to be easier than she'd anticipated.

Teach—Don't Punish!

From the beginning, the odds were stacked in favor of housetraining success with this puppy. The situation was ideal: The pup's dam was a good mother and teacher, the breeder was knowledgeable and diligent, and the new owner was watchful and well prepared. The dam started her pup's housetraining education, the breeder furthered it, and the new owner continued in a way that helped the pup succeed. If every breeder and new owner did their homework as thoroughly as in our story, there'd be very few housetraining problems.

But there are. Chances are if you picked up this book, you are having some of those problems. In addition, it's important to remember that even pups with the best possible start in housetraining have accidents. It *will* happen with every dog in every household.

In life there are many challenges, but housetraining a puppy or adult dog, though challenging at times, doesn't need to be difficult or frustrating. Often, all that's needed to prevent or solve elimination problems is some experienced guidance and a few new tricks. This book is written to provide you with both. Once you understand your dog's natural needs and inclinations, the housetraining process will be surprisingly quick and simple.

Punishment Is Ineffective

When those inevitable accidents do happen, please remember that punishment is not an effective tool for housetraining. Many pups will react to punishment by hiding future puddles and poops where the owner won't find them right away—behind the couch or under the desk,

It's your job to be patient with your puppy and anticipate his needs.

for example. This eventually may lead to punishment after the fact, which leads to more pee and poop hiding, and so on.

Instead of punishing your pup for potty accidents, stay a step ahead of mistakes by learning to anticipate his needs. Know your pup's natural elimination schedule—keep a written log if necessary. Learn to recognize the postures and actions your pup displays when he's getting ready to urinate or defecate. Then, instead of sending him out to his potty place alone, accompany him to the designated area when it's time to go. Calmly tell your pup what you want him to do; teach him a cue to eliminate (say something like "go potty" or "hurry hurry"). Wait patiently with your pup and praise him when he goes. This will work wonders; not only will he have the natural pleasure of relief, he'll know you're happy with his behavior. Punishment won't be necessary.

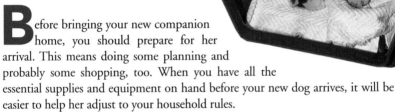

Chapter 2

A Housetraining Shopping List

Before bringing your new companion home, you should prepare for her arrival. This means doing some planning and probably some shopping, too. When you have all the essential supplies and equipment on hand before your new dog arrives, it will be easier to help her adjust to your household rules.

Supplies, equipment, and setup will vary somewhat, depending on the age of your new dog and her previous housetraining experience. A young puppy will demand more time and attention and will need to eliminate more often than an older pup or an adult dog. Puppies usually also require more supplies than adults, especially for those "accident" cleanups. Be sure you have plenty of everything you'll need to start your dog off right.

Equipment and Supplies

What's black and white and wet all over? This riddle is easy for new puppy owners: newspaper!

Newspaper

Reusing newspaper was popular among dog breeders and puppy owners long before recycling became a household word. A tall stack of newspapers is a handy resource for anyone trying to housetrain a puppy. Newspaper has many virtues—it's absorbent, abundant, cheap, and convenient. A section of the average daily news can soak up a good-sized puddle.

Be sure to have plenty on hand. The rule on sufficient newspaper supply is: The younger your puppy and the larger the breed, the more newspapers you'll need.

Puddle Pads

If you prefer not to stockpile newspaper, a commercial alternative is available. Thick, absorbent paper pads backed with a sheet of plastic can be purchased at pet supply stores under several trade names. Some are scented with an odor that attracts pups to use them. These puddle pads have the advantage of being waterproof, so urine doesn't seep through onto the floor. Their disadvantages are that they cost more than newspaper and contain plastic that isn't biodegradable.

> **CAUTION**
>
> **Newspaper Ink**
>
> Years ago, the ink used for printing newspapers contained lead and other toxic metals that were dangerous if ingested. Today, most (though not all) newspapers are printed with nontoxic vegetable-based inks. Some of the colorful advertising inserts, however, may still be printed with metal pigments, so to be on the safe side don't use those pages for housetraining. The black-and-white sections are not only safer, they're more absorbent.

This dog is ready for housetraining, with a crate, a penned area, and puddle pads. Puddle pads (to the left of the crate) are backed with plastic, which adds extra protection for your floors.

Litter Box and Litter

If your pup is a breed that remains small for life, you might consider using a litter box for her as an indoor potty spot. This can be either a temporary or a permanent arrangement, depending on your needs. When choosing a litter box, get one with sides low enough that your pup can easily hop in and out and large enough that wastes will end up inside the box and not on the floor next to it. Litter that's made of extruded pellets usually works better for dogs than the sand or gravel type made for cats, because it doesn't stick to paws and get tracked out of the box.

Potty Bell

One special piece of equipment that can make housetraining easier for both you and your dog is a bell on a cord. Hang this bell at dog nose level from the handle of the door you use for taking your pup out to her potty area. Each time you take your dog outside to eliminate, ring the bell just before you open the door. The sound of the bell soon becomes linked in the dog's mind with the opening of that door. Before long, she'll try ringing the bell herself, hoping to make the door open.

When you hear that bell ring, come a-running! Praise your dog and open the door. If your dog rings and you don't arrive to open the door, she may give up and potty right there.

A potty bell can be a single bell on a string or a several attached to a strip of cloth or leather, like sleigh bells. Be sure your bell is loud enough to hear a room or two away. Ringing a potty bell to go outside is one of the handiest tricks a dog can know.

Confining Your Pup

To housetrain a puppy, you'll need some way to confine her when you're unable to supervise. With one or more baby gates, a folding exercise pen, and a dog crate, you'll be able to socialize your pup and teach her good habits while keeping her out of trouble.

Baby Gates

Be sure the baby gates you use are safe. The old-fashioned expanding lattice type of gate has seriously injured many children by collapsing and trapping their legs, arms, fingers, and necks, and that type of gate can be just as dangerous for puppies. These gates have been officially recalled by manufacturers, but they're still around—in attics and basements, flea markets and garage sales. If you own this type of gate, don't trust it! Get one of the safer grid-style or vertical-slat baby gates instead.

Cleaning Up

Urine Cleanup

When dogs detect the scent of urine, they'll often mark that spot repeatedly. Urine scent can be difficult to eradicate, so it's important to promptly and thoroughly clean up all housetraining accidents. Here are some tips to help with urine cleanup.

- Clean up accidents right away, so there's less time for scent to be absorbed into the floor covering.
- To clean and diminish pet urine smell, use a household spray cleaner followed by white vinegar, applied liberally then mopped dry.
- Enzymatic cleaners can remove the scent of urine so dogs are no longer attracted to the spot.
- Don't use cleaners that contain ammonia. Ammonia is one of the ingredients that give urine its scent and may make the cleaned spot even more enticing to your dog.
- If the puddle is on carpeting, blot up the surface moisture, then lay absorbent materials (towels, rags, paper towels) on the spot and apply pressure to bring up urine that has soaked in deeper.
- Before using unfamiliar cleaning products on carpets, test a hidden spot first to be sure it won't stain or bleach.
- Watch your dog for several days after you've cleaned up an accident to make sure she doesn't urinate there again.
- Urine glows under black (ultraviolet) light. A battery-powered black light unit, available from pet supply stores, can make finding those dried urine spots easy.

Poop Pick-Up

Keep your dog's potty area picked up so it doesn't become an unpleasant place for her to walk. When an area becomes too soiled, many dogs will refuse to use it. Poop should be picked up daily to keep the chore from becoming overwhelming and also to visually check the dog's droppings. The color, consistency, and number of your dog's bowel movements can give you early warnings of many health problems.

Several styles of poop scoop tools are available. Some have two separate handles with a pan on one to hold droppings and a rake or hoe on the other to scoop with. (Hoes work well on concrete and packed soil; rakes are best for grass, gravel, or loose dirt.) Some scoops have handles hinged together like scissors. Some scoops need two hands to operate; others are made for one-handed use. To determine which style works best for you, try a dry run at your pet supply store. Put a handful of pebbles or small dog biscuits on the floor and pick them up with each type of scoop. Yard scooping can be quick and easy with the right tool.

Waste Disposal

Check your local laws concerning disposal of animal waste. In most areas you can bag it and throw it in the trash, but some cities ban dog and cat feces from household garbage or require double bagging or other special disposal.

If you have a house with a yard where you can dig a hole, you could bury the poop. Many shrubs appreciate dog poop as fertilizer when it's buried near their roots. It's considered unwise to put pet waste in a vegetable garden though, as some parasites can affect both animals and people.

An in-ground dog-waste digester is another option if you have a yard where you can dig a hole a couple of feet deep and wide. This is an open-bottomed plastic or metal cylinder buried a couple of feet in the ground, with a lid just above ground level to keep weather out and odors in. You'll need to periodically sprinkle special enzymes (available where digesters are sold) over the droppings to speed decomposition and convert the waste into soil.

Public Courtesy

When you and your dog visit parks or take walks around the neighborhood you'll need another poop-scooping accessory: plastic bags. Many cities and towns have laws about cleaning up pet waste in public areas—but even if yours doesn't, it's the right thing to do. Cleaning up after our dogs is a responsibility that must be taken seriously if we hope to keep our public dog-walking privileges intact.

Picking up after your dog using a plastic bag as a scoop is simple. Just put your hand inside the bag like a mitten, grab up the droppings, turn the bag inside out, and tie off the top. It's not very aesthetic, but it gets the job done.

Several companies sell special bags for poop pick-up. Some have a flat cardboard hoe with a plastic bag attached. Others have cardboard jaws. Some are scented with perfume; others are plain. Ordinary plastic food bags work just as well for poop pick-up as specialty scoop-bags.

Baby gates are a good way to keep puppies out of trouble.

Exercise Pens

Portable folding exercise pens, also known as ex-pens, are great for young pups or small dogs. These freestanding metal or plastic enclosures are made of rectangular panels that are hinged together. The pens are sturdy and can be folded and carried like a suitcase or easily stored when not in use. Set one up in your kitchen as the pup's daytime corral, and then take it outdoors for your pup to play in while you wash the car, work in the garden, or just sit and enjoy the day. Ex-pens are freestanding, but for safety it's best to fasten one side to something heavy that can't be tipped over.

Indoor Setup

A pup or dog who hasn't finished housetraining should never—repeat, never—be allowed the run of the house unattended. A new dog, especially a pup, with unlimited access to your whole home will, through no fault of her own, wreak havoc. If you let your pup or new dog roam your house without watching her, she'll leave urine puddles and poop piles in her wake. Prevention is the best solution, so set up a safe, comfortable, controlled environment for your new pet.

Socialization Considerations

The kitchen is usually a good place for a puppy's home base. Set up your pup's ex-pen there, if possible. Kitchens almost always have waterproof or easily cleaned floors, which is a distinct asset with a leaky pup. A bathroom, laundry room, or enclosed porch could be used as a puppy corral, but the kitchen is generally the best location because it's the hub of activity for many families. Corralled in the kitchen, a pup becomes accustomed to many sounds, sights, and smells, has an opportunity for human contact and learning approved behavior, and won't become lonely or bored.

Protecting Your Home

If your kitchen is small, a baby gate blocking the doorway can turn it into a fine puppy corral. If the kitchen is large, a portable exercise pen may work better because you can section off a smaller area of the room for your pup. An exercise pen can keep your pup away from cabinets, the stove, and other interesting but dangerous spots.

Even with vinyl flooring, you might wish to further protect your kitchen from puddles and other puppy damage. This can be done by first putting down a piece of heavy plastic sheeting, then a sheet of plywood. On top of the plywood, you can then spread your newspapers for the pup. This extra protection can be removed after your pup is housetrained.

Protecting Your Puppy

Pups are incredibly curious and will eat almost anything they can find. Keep this in mind as you puppy-proof all the areas where your pup will spend time alone. Floor-level kitchen cabinets, especially those under the sink, often hold caustic cleaners and other poisons.

Electrical cords are a common danger for pups; chewing one can have fatal results. Plug your appliances into counter-high outlets if you can, or block the pup's access to plugs near the floor. Make certain no electrical cords dangle temptingly where your pup could reach them—she might tug one and pull a hot or heavy appliance down onto herself.

When you think you've cleared away all the hazards, get down on your hands and knees to puppy eye level and take another look. You may be surprised what you'll see from a dog's point of view.

Laying Out the Pup's Area

When you first get your pup, spread newspaper over the whole floor of her playpen corral. Lay the papers at least four pages thick and be sure to

A gate blocking the doorway will keep a puppy confined to one room—if the pup is small or not an agile breed. Make sure the confinement method you choose will actually contain your pup.

Overusing a Crate

A crate serves well as an overnight bed, but don't leave your pup crated for more than a few hours during the day. Your puppy needs to play and exercise, which a crate does not allow. She also needs to drink water during the day and eliminate. Being deprived of sufficient water or holding her urine too long can both cause urinary tract problems.

A pup confined all day will probably start soiling her crate, which is not only unpleasant for both you and the dog, but causes her to learn bad cleanliness habits. If you must leave your dog confined for more than four hours, use a safely fenced outdoor area or an indoor ex-pen instead of a crate, so there's room for a bed, toys, a water bowl, and a potty area.

overlap the edges. Gradually decrease the size of the papered area until only the end where you want the pup to eliminate is covered. As you decrease the size of the "target" papers, be sure to leave enough so that the pup doesn't accidentally miss and wet the floor.

The way you structure your pup's area is very important. The bed, food, and water should be at the opposite end of the pup's corral from her potty area. If you will be training your dog to eliminate outside, place her indoor potty papers at the end of the corral closest to the door that leads to the outdoor area. That way, as she moves away from the clean area to the toilet area, the pup will form the habit of heading toward the door when she needs to eliminate.

The Importance of Scent

Until your pup gets the hang of using potty papers, help her remember where to go with a scent clue. When you clean up her potty area, keep a small soiled piece of the paper. Place this piece, which has the scent of her urine, under the top sheet of clean papers you spread. The scent of the soiled paper will cue your pup where to eliminate. When the pup needs to go potty, she'll search around for that scent and urinate near it. You will barely be able to smell it yourself, but your pup will have no trouble at all finding the right spot.

Outdoor Setup

Fences

If you are one of the fortunate dog owners with a yard or patio that can be safely fenced as an outdoor space for your pup, try to arrange your setup so you can let your pup out into the fenced yard directly from her indoor area. A fenced yard that is accessible from the pup's indoor area through an open door or a pet door will greatly facilitate the housetraining process. The fewer rooms your pup must pass through between her indoor corral and the outdoor potty area, the easier it will be for her.

Outside in your own yard or outside in a public place, you'll need to pick up after your dog. A pooper scooper can be handy.

Tie-Outs

Fences are safer for dogs than tie-outs. However, there are times and places where a fence is not an option and some other form of confinement must be used. Be aware that tying or chaining a dog can be very dangerous. A dog can become fatally entangled in her rope or cable. An overhead trolley tie-out tangles less than other types and is probably the safest tethering option, but these can still injure or even kill an unattended dog.

Plastic-covered metal cable makes a safer tie-out than chain and cannot be chewed through like rope. Fasten the tie-out just outside your door so it's handy to clip your dog to when she needs to eliminate. For your convenience, you should be able to reach the cable from the doorway so you can let your dog in and out without having to leave the house. Save yourself and your pup some misery and don't put her tie-out where it can tangle around bushes, trees, or lawn furniture.

If you use the tie-out only for the time it takes your dog to eliminate, you'll probably have no serious problems, but your dog should never be tied and left alone.

Laying Out the Pup's Yard

When setting up your pup's outdoor yard, put the bed and food/water area as far as possible away from the toilet area, just as with the indoor corral setup. Clean up droppings at least once a day, but leave one poop in the potty area to remind your dog where the right spot is. If there's too much poop on the ground, your dog won't want to walk through it and will start eliminating elsewhere.

Dogs are social creatures. They need people, dog friends, activity, training, and play. Isolation causes dysfunctional behaviors, such as excessive barking, digging, and aggression. Bring your dog into your home when you're there. Give her quality attention every day. The more time your dog spends with you, the better behaved, smarter, and more enjoyable a companion she will be.

Chapter 3

The First
Two Days

At last the big day has arrived! It's time to bring home your new dog. You've been carefully preparing for the pup's arrival. You've fenced in a potty yard outside and put up baby gates in your kitchen doorways to make a safe puppy corral with a comfortable dog crate, tip-proof water bowl, and several safe chew toys. Your cupboards are filled with high-quality dog food and treats.

Homecoming

Whether or not your new dog is crate-trained, he'll be safest in the car if he's riding in a crate, so be sure to take the crate with you when you go to pick up your pup. Inside his new crate/den, your pup will be less distracting to you while you drive and won't create dangerous situations in the car.

At first your pup might object to his crate if he's never been in one before. Give him something yummy to chew while he's in the crate and the pup will calm down and worry less about being confined.

A molded plastic crate is usually best for car travel because its strength and rigidity protect the dog in case of sudden stops or sharp turns. Molded plastic crates are more solid and quieter than the wire type, so they're cozier for the dog, too. If your pup eliminates or gets carsick on the way home, the mess probably won't leak out of a plastic crate, but lay some towels around it, just in case.

A crate sized for a pup or small dog will fit on the seat of most cars. If you're transporting your dog alone, place the crate in the front seat where you'll be able to comfort the pup without looking away from the road. Strap the crate in with the passenger seat belt. Face the door of the crate toward you, so your puppy can watch you drive instead of viewing the scenery whizzing toward the windshield. This can help prevent motion sickness. If you have another person with you, secure the crate in the back seat and have them sit back there with the pup to keep him company.

Travel Gear

Parents of young children sling along a diaper-bag stuffed with kid equipment wherever they go, and your puppy's necessities will require a similar bag. Be sure you have a leash, drinking water and bowl, biscuits and/or dry dog kibble, chew toys, plastic bags for poop pick-up, a roll of paper towels, a flashlight, and a first-aid kit with supplies for people and pets. Truly prepared dog owners also keep in the car some spray cleaner, old towels, and a package of disposable wet wipes for cleaning their hands and sometimes the puppy's rear. Toting a few extra things you might not use is better than being caught without those needed supplies.

On your way home, stop for a potty break after every thirty minutes of travel.

Potty Break

If you live more than an hour from the place you adopt your dog, his first lesson in elimination manners will be on the drive home. Stop for a potty break after about thirty minutes of travel—sooner if the pup is very restless.

When you stop, leash your dog before letting him out of the car. He doesn't know you yet and you really don't know him either, so don't give him a chance to run off and get lost or injured. Leash him.

Allow your pup a chance to walk around and stretch his legs. He may need to urinate or defecate, so give him ample opportunity for that. After the pup eliminates, talk to him and pet him. The bonding process has begun, and although you may have met this pup only

Immunization Concerns

Young pups who have not had their immunizations are at risk if they are exposed to canine diseases. Public areas such as parks, where many dogs are walked, can be hazardous for incompletely immunized pups. Germs may lurk in the grass or on the pathways. Walk your unprotected pup only in less-used areas and keep him away from any dog feces you might see.

Up-to-date immunizations, along with a good diet, plenty of water, exercise, and rest are the surest ways to keep your pup in the peak of health. Follow your veterinarian's advice on a schedule of immunization shots for your pup.

hours earlier, right now you're the most familiar face in his universe. Let everything you do show your new dog that you're his trustworthy friend who will take care of all his needs.

After his potty and petting break, return to the area where your pup eliminated and calmly encourage him to go again. He may or may not need to, but offer him the chance. After a minute or so, load him into the car again and head for home.

First Impressions

When you first arrive home with your new pup, take the urine-scented paper you brought from his former home and rub the scent in the area you've selected as an elimination place for him. If you'll be training the pup to eliminate outdoors, pour half a cup of lukewarm water through the urine paper and let the water seep into the ground. Don't leave the paper there though, or your pup will think it's something to play with.

The first day with a new dog is a very exciting time for the whole family. The pup has met you, but on arriving home everyone else will be excited to meet and pet and play with him. Try to keep the welcome fairly calm. Keep an eye on the pup and take him to his potty place before he has an accident in the house. Help him succeed by taking him to his potty area several times during the first few hours he's home, and then at least once every two hours until you've learned his elimination rhythms.

Too Much Excitement = No Elimination

Behave calmly when you take your puppy to his potty area. Too much chatter or overly enthusiastic praise will cause him to tense his muscles and not finish eliminating. When he calms down again after you've brought him back into the house, he may realize he didn't finish at the potty area. This means he'll need to go out again very soon.

Introducing the Potty Area

Take your pup on leash to his new potty area. Indicate the spot you've scented with his urine and encourage him to sniff around there. The familiar odor will give him a clue that this is the place to go. (If you're unable to scent a spot for your pup, just stand there patiently and wait for him to make his own mark.)

Take your pup outside frequently to eliminate. You may have to carry him there to prevent an accident.

Keep your new dog leashed so he won't wander away. Stand quietly and let him sniff around the designated area. If he starts to leave before he has eliminated, gently lead him back and remind him to go. If your pup sniffs the scented spot, praise him calmly and just wait. If he produces, praise serenely, then give him time to sniff around a little more. He may not be finished yet.

Take your pup to his potty place frequently throughout the day. Each time you successfully anticipate elimination and help your pup to the potty spot, you'll move another step closer to your goal. If you don't guide him carefully during the first couple of weeks, your new dog's understanding of housetraining rules will suffer.

Don't fret if your pup doesn't eliminate every time you take him to his potty area. Just familiarize him with the approved place and give him sufficient opportunities to go there. Dogs can be easily housetrained without punishment by anticipating their needs and helping them form good habits.

The First Night

Most dogs, even young ones, will not soil their beds if they can avoid it. For this reason, a sleeping crate can be a tremendous help during housetraining. Being crated at night can help your pup develop the muscles that control elimination. He will also learn that you're alert to his needs both day and night.

Bedtime

Take your pup to his potty area just before bedtime. Stand there with him and wait until he produces. Be patient and calm. This is not the time to play or excite your dog. If he's excited, he not only won't eliminate, he probably won't want to sleep when you bring him back in.

After your dog has emptied his bladder and bowels for the night, calmly put him to bed. The best place for your new dog's sleeping crate is near your own

---

Teach a Potty Cue

Yes, you can teach your puppy a verbal cue to eliminate. It doesn't matter what word or phrase you choose, just pick something you can say in public without embarrassment. Words or phrases like "go potty" or "do your business" work for many people, though some folks prefer more cryptic cues, such as "park."

Whatever cue word you select, use it consistently when you take your dog to the potty area. After he eliminates, reward him with calm praise that includes the cue word, as in "good go potty" or "good park." Soon your dog will associate that word with the act and will eliminate when you tell him.

Be ready for some midnight walks, especially the first few days. Remember, your puppy is a baby and lacks the physical development to hold his urine for a long time.

bed. Dogs are pack animals and they feel safer sleeping with others in a common area. In your bedroom the pup will be near you, so he'll sleep better. Also, if he wakes during the night and needs to eliminate, you'll be close enough to hear him and take him to his potty place.

Mid-Sleep Outing

Pups under four months of age often cannot hold their urine all night. If your puppy has settled down to sleep but a few hours later wakes and fusses, he very likely needs to go out. For best housetraining progress, take your pup to his elimination area whenever he needs to go, even when he wakes up in the wee hours of the morning.

Your pup may soil in the crate if you ignore his late-night urgency. It's unfair to let this happen and it sends the wrong message about your expectations for cleanliness. Resign yourself to this mid-sleep outing and just get up and take the pup to potty. Your pup will outgrow this need soon, so you won't have to do it forever.

The Second Day

This will be your first full day with your new dog, so start off immediately when you wake up. Take your pup to the potty area and tell him his cue to eliminate (see the box on page 33). After he eliminates, reward with praise that includes the cue word, such as "good potty" or "good hurry."

After your pup empties out, give him breakfast. Let him eat and drink until he's satisfied, then take him to his toileting area again. After that, he shouldn't need to eliminate again for a while, so you can allow him some playtime in the room with you or in his indoor corral. Keep an eye on the pup though, because if he pauses in play, he may need to go potty. Take him to the right spot, say the cue word, and praise him calmly if he produces. A young pup will sometimes fall asleep in the middle of playing. Don't wake him to take him out, but be sure you get him to his elimination area as soon as he wakes on his own.

Timing Is Everything

A pup under three months may need to urinate every hour and will move his bowels as many times a day as he eats. Once past four months, his potty trips will be less frequent.

Keep a chart of your new dog's potty behavior. Jot down what time he eats, sleeps, and eliminates. After several days a pattern will emerge that can help you determine your pup's body rhythms. Once you know your new dog's natural rhythms, you'll be able to anticipate his needs and schedule appropriate potty outings. Your dog will have a higher success rate this way, and that will speed up housetraining.

Food and Water

Nutritional needs are high in puppies, but their holding capacity is small, so they need to eat frequently. Pups younger than four months need three or four meals a day and free access to fresh drinking water. A dog's digestive system is closely allied with his elimination system; eating sets them both in motion. A pup will move his bowels about as many times a day as he eats, so frequent meals mean frequent elimination.

Your pup won't need water during sleeping hours, but make sure he has access to clean water all day long. Limiting the amount of water a dog drinks will not help with housetraining, and a lack of sufficient water can be dangerously unhealthy. A dog needs water to digest food, maintain proper body temperature and blood volume, and clean his system of toxins and wastes. A healthy dog will automatically drink the right amount. Do not restrict water intake.

Controlling your dog's access to water is not the key to housetraining, but controlling his access to everything else is.

> **TIP**
>
> **Elimination Times**
>
> When a puppy first awakens, when he pauses in play, and after he eats or drinks, he will need to eliminate. Always take your pup to his potty area at those times. Those are universal elimination times for all dogs, including mature adults.

The best way to deal with mistakes is to avoid them. Watch your pup carefully and make sure you get him outside often.

Watch Your Pup

Never allow your pup out of your sight, either indoors or out, unless he's securely enclosed in his crate or puppy corral. When you're not able to watch him, he will make his own choices. If he's free to roam your house, you can bet he'll choose inappropriate places to eliminate. Be watchful. Every potty mistake delays housetraining progress; every success speeds it along.

Chapter 4

Crate Training

The wild wolf makes her den big enough to turn around and lie down in, yet small enough that her own body heat can warm the space. Here she can retreat from danger and rest safely. The den is a private place, a place of security and serenity. No wolf would be happy without her den.

Domesticated dogs bear little physical resemblance to their wolf cousins, but most have a similar preference for cavelike dens. It's not unusual for a pet dog to retreat under a table or chair when she chews on a bone or takes a nap. That type of "cave" is the closest thing to a cozy den available in most modern homes.

Crate-Dens

There's a great den substitute for the modern dog that's even better than a real cave, because it's clean, comfortable, and portable. This modern cave is called a crate or travel kennel. A crate-den will provide your dog with a private sleeping and lounging area where she's not underfoot. It can also be a very useful house-training aid.

Crates are widely available—you can find them in any pet supply store or catalog. The two main types are folding wire crates and molded plastic crates. There are other crates too, made of sturdy fabric, wood, or sheet metal, but the plastic and wire models are generally the most useful for housetraining.

Plastic Crates

Molded plastic crates are made in two separate sections: top and bottom. These sections attach together with screws or built-in clips. Top and bottom sections can be nested for storage. The top section has ventilation holes along both sides, and the bottom section has solid sides that prevent drafts. There is a removable grated door made of metal or plastic that allows good airflow.

Inside a plastic crate both light and sound are subdued, making it a soothing environment for the dog. These crates don't rattle or squeak when the dog moves around, so they're not noisy while you are trying to sleep. The plastic crates are sturdy, secure, and easy to clean, and many are approved for airline travel.

Wire Crates

Wire crates are made of sturdy welded wire panels, hinged together to fold flat for storage. When the crate is set up, a shallow plastic or metal pan slides into the bottom. This gives the dog a smooth surface to lie on and helps contain dirt and wetness. Wire crates are easy to set up and take down and they'll store in a narrow space. They are not approved for air travel.

These crates are open all around to air and light. If a room is warm, this allows better air circulation than a plastic crate, but when the weather is cool a wire crate can be drafty. The wire panels tend to rattle when the dog moves around inside, which can be an annoying sound at night. The crate can be made quieter and less drafty by covering the top and sides with a towel or a blanket. Leave the front uncovered to allow ventilation and a view. Covering a wire crate also makes the space more private and cozy, which most dogs like.

If your pup has a potty accident in a wire crate, the bottom pan will keep wetness from seeping downward, but the mess may leak out the open sides. Cleaning a wire crate requires scrubbing each wire and welded junction individually and is more work than cleaning the same mess from a plastic crate.

Although both types of crates have advantages, all in all, plastic crates are most often the best choice for housetraining.

> **TIP**
>
> **Instant Bed**
>
> Once your dog is housetrained and reliable when he's not crated at night, you can remove the top and door of a plastic crate and use the bottom as a doggie bed. Or you can simply leave the crate door open all the time so your dog can come and go as she pleases. Leave a blanket or cushion in the bottom of the crate. Dirt and hair will collect there instead of blowing around the room, and the plastic easily washes clean of dirt and oils from the dog's coat.

Pups will investigate the crate with great curiosity.

Introducing the Crate

It may take a few days for your dog to get used to her crate, but once they're accustomed to it most dogs enjoy the cozy space. The first time a dog is closed in a crate, she doesn't know if she'll ever get out again. That can cause some anxiety, so it's best to let her get used to it with the door open at first.

Introduce the crate in as pleasant a manner as possible. Put the crate where your pup can explore it and tie the door open so it won't accidentally slam shut. Show your dog some very small (or broken-up) treats she especially likes and casually toss a few into the crate. Encourage her to go in and eat them, but don't make a big deal of it. Some dogs are nervous about going into a crate the first few times, while others will dash in without hesitation. Whichever approach your pup takes, be patient and stay calm. Don't try to pressure her, force her, or trick her into going in. It's best if you allow your pup to discover on her own that the crate is a safe and comfortable place.

After your pup has ventured in and out to eat treats a few times and isn't worrying about it anymore, toss in a small handful of treats, send her in after them, and quietly shut the door. Keep it shut just long enough to praise the pup, then open the door (whether she's finished eating the treats or not). Make a game of sending the pup in and out of the crate a few times, closing the door for gradually longer periods.

Alone in the Crate

When your pup will stay calm in the crate for about five minutes with you in sight, it's time for the next step. Put the pup in her crate with a food-stuffed chew toy or a safe bone, close the door, and busy yourself in the same room but out of her view. If she whines or seems anxious, say a few calm words now and then, as if you were talking to yourself, not the pup. This will let her know you're still there but won't give her any direct attention. Basically, ignore her for a few minutes. Then go back to her, praise her calmly, and let her out. Do this three times, then take a break.

Take her to her potty area as soon as you let her out, in case she needs to go. This is a good habit to get into: Always give your dog a chance to eliminate right away whenever you release her from confinement—whether from the crate, the house, or the car.

After she's relieved herself, spend some pleasant interactive time with her. Take a walk or play a game she enjoys that's not too rambunctious. Then give her some free time with you in the same room where the crate is. Leave the door of the crate open and her chew toy or bone inside where she can get it if she wants. Busy yourself quietly and don't pay any obvious attention to your pup. She may or may not go into the crate to get the chewie, and if she does, she'll decide either to stay there to chew it or take it out. Allow her that choice. If she does settle in the crate on her own, don't throw a party—just smile quietly to yourself.

Later that day or the next, put your pup in her crate with her food-stuffed toy or bone. Close the door and remain in the room until she's enjoying the bone or chew toy. Then leave the room for a minute. When you return to your pup, praise her calmly. If she seems happy chewing on her bone or toy, leave for ten to fifteen minutes, then return and let her out.

It's possible that instead of enjoying her chewie, your pup might fuss when you leave the room. If that happens, don't scold and don't apologize. Just stay out of sight for one minute, then go back to your pup as if everything were perfectly ordinary.

Check that the pup is OK and pet her with your fingers through the closed door. Then quietly tell her she's a good dog and leave the room again. If the pup stays quiet, wait one minute, return, praise, and let her out. If, instead of being quiet, she starts to bark or cry, wait until she stops for a moment. Then return to her and praise her calmly. Stand silently by the crate for about thirty seconds, then praise your pup, calmly open the crate, and let her out.

Repeat this lesson three times that day. Be sure she has a food-stuffed chew toy or bone in the crate with her, so there's something enjoyable for her to do to pass the time. Each session, leave the pup crated a few minutes longer. By the end of the day she should be able to stay calm and quiet in her crate for ten to fifteen minutes with you out of the room.

After spending a few short periods alone in her crate, she'll realize that you always come back and let her out. Most dogs soon become comfortable enough in their crates that they'll go in on their own when they want a private place to lounge or nap.

Nighttime Crating

A crate is a cozy, private bed for your dog. It will also keep her safe and out of mischief while you're sleeping. Before you close your dog in her crate for the night, be sure you take her out to eliminate one last time. You may have to wake your puppy to do this, but if you don't take the pup to eliminate

It may take a little while for your pup to settle down quietly in her crate. Be patient and reward the smallest successes.

before you go to bed, you'll have to take her later. Worse yet, the pup may wake and whine and you might sleep right through her pleas. If this happens, you're sure to wake up to a mess.

If you put your pup's crate in your bedroom at night, she will feel more secure because she's near you. Also, with her in your bedroom you're more likely to hear her if she wakes up and needs to eliminate in the middle of the night.

Daytime Crating

When you're home during the day, your dog should spend as much time with you as possible. A good way to keep her from wandering off to eliminate on the rug is to tie her leash to your belt. Let her follow you around like a shadow. When you walk, she walks. When you stop, she stops. When you stand at the sink to wash dishes or sit at your computer desk answering e-mail, the pup lies on the floor by your feet. Keeping her with you like this makes it impossible for her to do anything wrong without you noticing and redirecting her.

> ## Midnight Potty Break
>
> Get up when your pup wakes you at night and take her to the elimination area. The fewer accidents you let your pup have, day or night, the sooner her housetraining will be complete. Each time the pup uses her designated potty area, she mentally links that place with relief and praise. Memories of success accumulate, and when your pup feels the urge to go, she'll remember where she went before. Each successful incident helps the pup form the clean habits you want her to have. Final result: clean dog, happy owner.

When you are unable to supervise for an hour or so, put your pup in her crate to nap or chew on a bone. Always give her the chance to eliminate before closing her in her crate, and when you release her, take her immediately to her potty area.

Alternative Confinement Options

If your pup must be alone all day, don't leave her in the crate. The crate is only big enough to comfortably sleep in. At night that's fine—in fact, that's exactly what you want—but during the day a dog has different needs. There isn't enough space in a crate to meet those needs. There's no room to play and no place to eliminate. If you must be gone more than four hours, an indoor pen or a puppy-proofed room is the solution.

If you have a fenced yard with good shelter for the pup, you might leave her outdoors in mild weather instead of in the house. But make sure the fence is secure so your pup can't escape and other animals (and people) can't get in and harm her. It's risky leaving a puppy unattended outdoors, even in a fenced yard. Dangers include poisonous plants, insects, snakes, teasing kids, and dognappers. Even if you have a lovely yard for your pup, she may be safer in the house when nobody is home.

Safety Check from a Pup's-Eye View

A puppy-safe room or indoor corral must be safety-checked before leaving the pup alone. A bored puppy can be very destructive, so make sure your pup's corral will actually keep her out of trouble. Get down on your hands and knees with your eyes at the same level as your pup's. Now look around. The scenery is different; you're seeing things from your pup's point of view.

Do you see anything that sticks out or hangs down? Your pup will want to chew or pull on those items, so either move them or block the pup's access to them. Move any precious keepsakes to higher ground or to another room until your pup grows into a dignified adult. Keep temptations to a minimum while your pup is immature.

Setting Up the Pup's Corral Area

Put the pup's bed, food, water, and toys at one end of the corral area. At the opposite end, spread overlapping newspapers or puddle pads to serve as the potty area. Your pup will gradually start eliminating farther from her bed and food, and you'll be able to clear away the papers between the lounging area and the potty area.

Until your pup is housetrained, she shouldn't be allowed to roam the house on her own. There will be times you can't watch her though, even when you're home. Her puppy corral will come in handy at those times. If it's in the kitchen or another busy part of the house, she can spend time there without being isolated from the family. This is important, because a developing pup needs lots of social interaction and attention.

Wrongful Crating

It's unfair to crate a puppy for the night and then lock her up again all day while you go to work. A crate-den is a safe and cozy bed, and can be a big help during housetraining, but it is not a storage unit. You can unwittingly cause serious behavior and health problems by overusing the crate.

The general rule for daytime crate use is no more than one hour of crate time per day for each month of a pup's age (up to five months). In other words, a three-month-old dog should not spend more than a *total* of three daytime hours in a crate—and that time is best broken up into smaller increments. And no dog of any age should be left in a crate longer than four to five hours during the day.

Part II

Making Housetraining Easy

Chapter 5

Age-Appropriate Housetraining

I t's truly amazing how fast a puppy grows and develops. The helpless canine infant turns into a chubby toddler at about five weeks, a playful buddy at six weeks, a little explorer by seven, and is ready to conquer his new home between eight and twelve weeks of age. Time flies, but sometimes it may seem as if you've been mopping up after your puppy for ages. Don't worry; the situation will improve each week as your pup develops better control of his body.

Baby Puppy (4 to 7 Weeks)

Puppies, like human babies, need time to develop their bodies and minds before they can control their elimination. The younger your pup, the longer it will be before he'll be fully housetrained. Keep your expectations appropriate for his age.

4 Weeks

At 4 weeks old, a pup should still be with his mama. He needs his mother's company, body heat, and nurturing guidance. A 4-week-old puppy still needs to nurse and may not yet have eaten solid food. Four weeks is simply too young to adopt a puppy unless he has no mother to nurture and protect him and you're willing to take on the care and feeding of an infant canine.

At 4 weeks, a pup is too young to grasp the concept of housetraining. He will stay close to his bed and food source and will eliminate wherever he happens to be when nature calls. This is not a lack of cleanliness; at this age his eliminative functions are not really under his voluntary control. Bowel and bladder control develop gradually.

The best "housetraining" tactic with a puppy this young is to train yourself to deal with the situation. Spread plenty of newspaper or puddle pads on the floor of the pup's area.

5 Weeks

At about 5 weeks old, a pup can begin to eat solid foods. The mother dog may still nurse her litter, but she no longer cleans up their wastes. Instead, after nursing the dam leads her pups a short distance from the den to eliminate. A puppy with a good mother receives early training in clean habits that way.

Five-week-old puppies should stay with their mama at least two more weeks. During that period, the mother dog finishes weaning her pups and will teach them a few doggie social graces—such as eliminating a distance away from the eating area. If you're housetraining a 5-week-old pup, you'll need to take him to his potty place at lease once an hour, and sometimes more frequently. This is so time-consuming that it usually isn't practical. The best solution may be to spread papers over the entire puppy corral floor and wait a few weeks before trying to start housetraining.

Baby puppies cannot control their eliminations. All you can do is cover the floor with lots of newspaper and take them out frequently.

6 Weeks

When a pup reaches 6 weeks of age, it's still early to expect much bladder and bowel control. You can, however, begin housetraining a puppy this age, though the "training" will mainly consist of you learning to take the infant to his potty spot before he makes a mess.

At 6 weeks, a pup may still need hourly opportunities to eliminate at certain times of day. Get to know your pup's body rhythms by charting his elimination for several days. That will give you a rough idea of your pup's daily cycles and help you anticipate his potty needs.

7 Weeks

At about 7 weeks of age, when a pup feels the urge to eliminate he'll try to do it away from his food and bedding areas. This behavior signals developmental readiness to begin housetraining. The puppy will still need to eliminate every hour or two, but with guidance he can begin to understand that there is an approved place for this.

Early on, housetraining means you learning to take the infant to his potty spot before he makes a mess.

When your pup defecates most of the time toward the far end of his corral, away from his food and bed area, you can begin to shift the newspapers toward that end. Widen the gap between the pup's bedding and papers by a few inches each day. Don't uncover too much floor between the bed and the potty area too suddenly or your puppy may not know where he's supposed to eliminate. If he thinks the papers have suddenly disappeared entirely, he'll do his business on the uncovered floor, which can start a bad habit. Gradual change works best at this stage, so make it easy for your pup to understand where he's supposed to go.

As a puppy matures, he develops control of his bowels first, then his bladder. At 7 weeks, most pups have begun to gain some control. But don't expect any housetraining miracles yet. Your pup may still sometimes urinate wherever he happens to be when the urge strikes and then go back to playing as if nothing had happened. This is natural and innocent, so don't get upset with him. Just learn to be watchful so you can help him remember where he's supposed to go.

At about 7 weeks, your pup can start learning a word for elimination. Having an actual cue or command

> ### T I P
>
> **The Best Age to Get a Pup**
>
> Only in cases of dire necessity should a puppy be taken from his dam before 6 weeks of age. The period between 8 and 12 weeks is generally considered a better time for a puppy to go to his permanent home. By that age, the pup has learned about dog social behavior from mama and his siblings and is ready to start bonding with a human family.

to go potty can be extremely handy. A potty cue makes it easier for you to control where and when your dog eliminates. You'll be able to take your pup to his spot and say the potty cue, and he'll get right down to business.

Young Puppy (8 to 15 Weeks)

An 8-week-old puppy may still need to eliminate every two to three hours when he's awake, and more often if he's playing vigorously and drinking water to cool off. Keep in mind the four key times a pup needs to eliminate: after waking, eating, drinking, and playing (or other exciting events). Take your pup to the elimination spot at those times and any other time he acts as if he might need to go (see the box on page 52).

Eight-week-old pups get some warning before they must eliminate, and they'll usually try to do it away from their bed and food. At this stage you can continue decreasing the size of the papered area in the pup's corral. Put newspapers at the opposite side of the corral from the bed, food, and water, so they are two distinct areas. If possible, locate the papers at the end of the pen that's closest to the door leading outside. The pup will get used to walking toward that door when he needs to eliminate, which begins a pattern that's part of housetraining.

Pups develop habits quickly, so make sure the habits your puppy develops are good. The more times each day your pup eliminates in the approved area, the faster his housetraining will proceed. Help him form good habits by being attentive and guiding him appropriately.

Puppies form habits very quickly, so make sure your pup forms the right habits. Take him out frequently and he'll soon understand that outside is the place to eliminate.

Each time you take your pup to his potty spot, quietly tell him the cue you've chosen for elimination. Praise softly as he goes, including the cue in your praise. Soon your pup will recognize the elimination cue and you'll be able to tell him where and when to do his business.

The Potty Bell

Now it's time to introduce the potty bell I described in chapter 2. Hang a bell, a wind-chime, or a string of sleigh bells from the handle of the door that leads to the potty place. The bell should hang at puppy nose level so it's easy for your dog to see and reach. Be sure the bell is loud enough to hear from the next room. You won't always see your pup ring it, so you'll need to be able to hear it and open the door for him.

Don't worry about specifically training the pup to ring the bell. Just ring the bell yourself before you open the door each time you take him out to eliminate. The way a dog thinks, whatever precedes an event is the cause of the event. So if you ring the bell before opening the door, your pup will get the idea that ringing the bell causes the door to open. When he makes this connection, he will try ringing the bell so the door will open. When you hear the bell, hurry to the door to take your pup outside. Praise him for letting you know he has to go.

If you brought your pup home at 7 or 8 weeks of age, by 10 weeks he may already have learned to ring the potty bell when he needs to go out. He's probably also aware that there's a certain place to eliminate. The pup may have no idea how to get to that special spot without your help, though, so you should continue to escort your puppy to his potty area. That is the only way you can be sure he will form the good habits you want him to have, and you'll be right there to praise him for doing the right thing in the right place.

Previous Home Environment

If you adopt a pup 12 to 16 weeks of age who has been kept in a clean environment and educated by his mama about clean potty habits, you should have little trouble housetraining him. At this stage, a pup is aware of his need to eliminate far enough in advance that he has time to ask to go out. He won't always have perfect timing, though, so be patient and understanding. Continue to praise him for eliminating in the right place and also be sure to praise when your pup lets you know he needs to go.

If you adopt a pup of 12 to 16 weeks who has been kept in unsanitary quarters, he's already used to living that way and you'll have to work harder teaching him clean habits. Be patient, consistent, and compassionate. Give the pup time and you'll succeed in housetraining him.

A new pup from a deprived or dirty background will need a lot of attention. Although such a pup may be physically normal, he may not try to move away

---

The "Shadow" Leash

When your puppy is out of his corral, instead of letting him explore your house on his own and undoubtedly get into trouble, tether him to your waist with a six-foot leash. Make him your little shadow, so even if your attention isn't focused solely on him, he'll stay with you and out of mischief. He won't be able to wander off to eliminate in unapproved places or chew on inappropriate things. And because he's right there with you, you'll notice when he seems restless and might need to eliminate. You'll be right there to take him to his potty area and praise him when he goes. This will help him form clean habits.

Signals Your Dog Needs to Go

Your pup will display some characteristic behaviors when he feels the urge to eliminate. These tell-tale signals are your cue for action. Be alert, and when your pup starts to make these signals, take him immediately to his potty area. The younger your pup, the less time between his starting these behaviors and actually eliminating. Here are those important signs:

- Pup stops what he's doing and starts sniffing around anxiously.
- Pup suddenly stops what he's doing and walks away.
- Pup starts slowly walking in a circle.
- Pup starts spinning in a circle with a slightly hunched posture.
- Pup trots toward another room or steps behind a piece of furniture.
- Pup sniffs or acts interested in a spot where he's previously had a housetraining accident.

When your pup shows any of these signs that he's getting ready to eliminate, interrupt him in a friendly manner and escort him to his approved potty area.

from his bed and food before eliminating. This pup isn't used to having any part of his environment free of waste, so he has no idea that it makes a difference. You must be vigilant with this pup. Watch for his potty signals as carefully as you would watch a very young puppy. You'll learn your pup's potty signals and catch him in time—if you're on your toes. It may take longer than average for this pup to learn clean habits. On the other hand, a pup from a poorly managed environment may possibly be so happy to have a decent-smelling place to sleep and eat that he catches on very quickly.

Crate or Corral?

A pup can hold his urine for only about as many hours as his age in months. So a 2-month-old pup needs to urinate at least every two hours. At 4 months old he may be able to manage about four hours between piddles. Pups vary somewhat in their rate of development though, so this is not a hard and fast rule. It is, however, a realistic idea of how long a pup can be left without needing access to a potty place.

While crating for short periods can help a pup learn to control his bladder and bowels, being crated too long isn't healthy or kind. When a pup is forced to hold his urine longer than is natural, toxins can build up in his body and cause bladder infections or irritations. These unhealthy conditions can make housetraining nearly impossible. There are medications to heal these disorders, but it's much better and healthier not to cause them by over-crating your pup.

A crate may be used to confine a puppy for one or two hours, but use an indoor or outdoor pen if he must be left unattended for longer periods. Confine your puppy in a portable folding exercise pen or

Be patient with your pup and remember that he wants to please you.

other puppy-safe corral with room to play and newspapers for elimination. The pup will be able to maintain his healthy, natural body rhythms without using the rest of your home as his toilet. If he has the opportunity to eliminate only in approved areas, the pup won't be confused about where to go and will be house-trained sooner.

Older Puppy (4 to 6 Months)

By 4 months of age, most puppies have fairly good bladder and bowel control. They usually are aware that they need to eliminate far enough in advance to ask to go to the designated elimination area and enough time to get there. By 4 to 6 months, a pup raised with a potty bell will be ringing it to notify his owners when he needs to go out. The pup may not be fully housetrained yet, but he's getting close.

If you adopt a pup this age, hopefully he's already had introductory house-training at his former home. If the pup has been raised and kept in a clean environment with access to a potty area, he may already have the right idea. If you're lucky, he might be almost fully housetrained.

On the other hand, if you adopt a pup this age who has never had a chance to eliminate away from his living area, you should proceed with housetraining as if the dog was a very young pup. He will be able to hold his elimination for longer periods, but he has no more idea of the proper place to go than a baby pup would. Be very patient, vigilant, and positive with this puppy. He needs your help and support.

Adolescent Dog (7 to 12 Months)

At 7 months, a pup has nearly reached full growth and is close to attaining adult bladder and bowel control. With this maturity sometimes also comes a desire to mark territory. Adolescent and adult male dogs are especially likely to mark, but many females do too.

Urine and feces carry a dog's unique body scent. Dogs urinate and sometimes defecate to mark the borders of their yard and at regular checkpoints along daily walking routes. Some dogs scuff the ground with their hind feet, scratching the surface soil after marking the spot with urine or feces. This isn't to cover their mark; it's to emphasize it. A dog's paw pads have scent-producing areas, so scuffing leaves more odor and a visual mark as well.

When you walk an adolescent dog, it's a good tactic to curb his desire to mark repeatedly along the route. Marking is about turf, and a dog claims all the real estate he can by wetting it with urine. If he is allowed to do this at will, your dog may mark more and more frequently until he's stopping at every bush and blade of grass. Prevent this natural impulse from getting out of control by allowing your dog to urinate on walks only when you stop and tell him it's okay.

Some adult male dogs, if allowed to mark as often as they like, may take two hours to walk around one block. Don't misunderstand your adolescent dog's urge to urinate so frequently. The dog isn't going so often because he can't hold his bladder; he's actually rationing each squirt so he doesn't run out before he gets home. If he was only urinating for comfort, he could get the job done in one stop. It's okay to let your dog mark a few posts on your walk, but you won't create a hardship if you don't let him mark on every upright surface along the way.

Adult Dog (1 to 7 Years)

A healthy adult dog can control his eliminative functions about as well as most adult humans. During adulthood, there are seldom any problems with elimination control unless the dog is ill or injured. Medical and environmental conditions can affect elimination in an adult dog, so if an elimination problem suddenly shows up, take your dog to the veterinarian for a thorough checkup.

Moving to a New Home

A common non-medical cause for an adult dog to break house-training is a move to a new home. Until a dog can adjust to his new surroundings, there may be a few potty accidents. As the dog settles in to his new territory, he may leave urine marks to register his claim on the new turf. By establishing a border of scent posts, the dog informs other animals that the area is now occupied.

Some dogs, while marking boundaries to prove ownership of a new property, may also try marking items inside the home. If this occurs, take your dog to the newly marked spot, indicate what he's done and calmly tell him "no" or "wrong." Then take him outside to a spot that's okay for him to mark and cue him to eliminate there. Praise if he marks the permitted spot. You may have to watch the dog carefully for several weeks in a new home to prevent him from marking in inappropriate places.

Senior Dog (7 Years and Older)

In his senior years, a dog's body gradually wears down. Sometimes certain body systems will suddenly deteriorate. Older dogs may begin to have less control of eliminative functions and occasionally become incontinent for one or more reasons. Illness or hormone imbalance may cause an older dog to break housetraining. Sometimes bladder or bowel muscles relax too much during sleep or exercise and some urine or feces leaks out. Whatever the cause, age-related incontinence is not intentional—it is a physical disability that must be humanely managed and cannot be trained away. If your senior dog begins having trouble with elimination, be compassionate and try to help as much as possible. Sometimes medication will help. Other cases are only helped by managing the dog and his environment.

A dog must *never* be punished for soiling when he cannot control himself—not as a little puppy and certainly not in his old age. Shaming an old dog for an unintentional breach in housetraining is insensitive and cruel. It might be upsetting to wake up or arrive home to a mess, but it's not the old dog's fault. The dog needs emotional support for this loss of dignity, not a scolding.

Changes in elimination habits can indicate health problems. Take your older dog in for a check-up if he's having problems. And never punish your old friend for housetraining mistakes.

Two items can help make life better for an incontinent dog: absorbent garments and special bedding. The garments are panties for female dogs and a belly band for the males. Both these types of garments have a pouch that holds a disposable or washable absorbent pad that wicks moisture away from the dog's skin but prevents it from leaking onto the floor or bedding. Bedding for incontinent dogs should be easily washable and include a top layer that wicks away moisture and a plastic-backed bottom layer that retains it.

If you notice your mature dog seems to have less control of his elimination than usual, take him to the veterinarian right away. He could be developing old-age incontinence, but he could also have a health problem that's unrelated to his age. In all likelihood, with help from your veterinarian you'll be able to make your dog comfortable and happy through his senior years.

Chapter 6

Paper Training

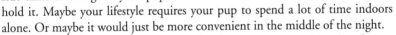

Sometimes it's handy to have a pup use an indoor elimination area. Maybe there's no safe nearby outdoor area. Maybe the elevator ride takes too long for your pup to hold it. Maybe your lifestyle requires your pup to spend a lot of time indoors alone. Or maybe it would just be more convenient in the middle of the night.

A papered surface may already be familiar to your pup from her former home, if her breeder provided newspapers for the puppies to eliminate on. If you do decide to train your pup to go in an indoor potty area, there are several suitable materials you can use.

Newspaper is abundant, absorbent, and free—a great combination for the purpose at hand. Newspaper sections can be opened to cover a large surface. They can soak up quite a large puddle and are easy to pick up when they are soiled.

One drawback to housetraining on newspaper is that the pup learns to seek out newspaper when she needs to eliminate. This can be a problem if someone drops the Sunday paper on the floor and leaves the room.

The other disadvantage to using newspaper as a potty area material is its smudginess. This is a very minor problem, because the ink easily washes off with soap and water. If you prefer to avoid the ink problem but still wish to paper-train your pup, it's sometimes possible to purchase a large roll of unused newsprint from your local newspaper or from a paper supply wholesaler. Since it has no ink, this paper creates no smudges. The rolled paper lacks one advantage of the printed, folded product: it must be torn off in big pieces and layered. The

Baby puppies cannot control their eliminations. All you can do is cover the floor with lots of newspaper and take out the pups frequently.

folded sections of printed newspaper are more convenient because they're uniform in size and several pages thick.

A convenient, though more expensive, alternative to newspaper is a commercial puppy puddle pad. There are several brands available at pet supply stores. The pads are made of absorbent layers of paper backed by a sheet of waterproof plastic.

Puddle pads are usually about half the size of a sheet of newspaper, which means you may need to spread several, overlapping them at the edges, to create a large enough target for your pup to hit. For this reason, doggie puddle pads are most suitable for small pups and toy breeds.

Hospital supply stores sell a similar product, normally used for incontinent patients. These come in larger sizes than puppy puddle pads and when purchased in bulk may be less expensive than the doggie version.

Where to Put the Papers

Even after they have mastered appropriate elimination behavior, most pups must still be confined when they are left alone to prevent trash raiding, furniture chewing, counter surfing, and other doggie misdemeanors.

Your pup's indoor corral will be in use for several months, so it should be in a convenient central location. In the kitchen, your pup will receive attention and training and feel like a member of the family. Moreover, a kitchen typically has a washable floor and often a door leading to an outdoor potty area.

Some dog owners use a bathroom, laundry room, mudroom, or porch for their pup's corral area. If this room is connected to the kitchen and is a high-traffic area, it may be suitable. However, if the room you choose for your pup's corral doesn't have much activity it is not a good place for your pup. A puppy tucked out of the mainstream receives less attention from people. This will slow her education and hold her back socially. An isolated pup won't see her owners as often as she should, won't get to play interactive games, won't be learning good manners, and won't be very happy.

A puppy needs socialization to become an attentive, obedient companion without abnormal fears or aggression. A lonely pup will tend to get into more mischief—she'll dig up the flooring for exercise. She'll bark and whine and chew the walls for entertainment. And she won't form that wonderful bond with you that's the greatest joy of living with a dog.

Setting Up Your Pup's Corral

Place your pup's bed or crate and her bowls and toys at the end of her corral farthest from the door to the outside. When she moves away from her bed to eliminate, she'll also be moving toward the door—part of a helpful pattern of learning if you also plan to teach your pup to eliminate outdoors.

Puppies are social creatures, and will not develop properly if they are isolated from your family.

When you first bring home your pup, cover the whole floor of her indoor corral, wall to wall, with newspaper or puddle pads. The pup will get used to eliminating on the paper and learn to seek that texture underfoot when she needs to eliminate. This kind of paper training is a convenient way to teach young pups there are approved places to eliminate; even little puppies can understand that only part of the world is covered with newspaper.

A very young pup will barely step away from her bed before eliminating. As her body matures, the puppy will walk farther from her sleeping nest to eliminate. When you notice your pup is eliminating several feet away from her bed, begin shrinking the newspaper area.

Start by leaving a narrow strip of bare floor between the pup's bed and the papers. This gap should be no wider than the pup's body length. It's important the pup understands she still should use the papers, but that she must cross bare floor to get to them. If the gap is too wide, the pup may miss the target and urinate on the uncovered floor. This causes the pup to practice the wrong behavior—which isn't what you want. Give your puppy every opportunity to be clean and she'll learn more quickly and reliably.

Safety

Check the space where you'll be confining your pup for potential dangers before you leave her alone there for even a moment. Check any floor-level cabinets to be certain the latches can't be opened by puppy paws or teeth. Put all electrical

Start by covering the entire corral with newspaper.

Surface Problem

A pup's potty behavior is connected to her tactile memory of the footing in the elimination area. This creates a challenge for a dog who has learned to eliminate on grass and now must switch to using a paved terrace or patio.

To help her out, temporarily give her some of the surface she's used to. A landscape company could provide you with a chunk of sod grass. Put the grass on your patio and teach your dog to eliminate there.

Over a period of a week or two, your dog's urine scent will seep down through the grass into its soil base. Remove the piece of sod but leave some of the urine-scented soil on the paved surface for a few more days. Once your dog is accustomed to using the spot without the sod on it, you'll soon be able to sweep away the soil and your dog will continue to eliminate in that area.

cords out of chewing range. Doors or gates to the puppy's area must close securely to prevent escape. Gates should lock into place yet be easily opened with one hand. Easy-open gates for doorways can be found at department stores, pet supply stores, and stores that sell items for children. Make sure the gate you choose really is escape-proof.

The Transition to Outdoors

To help a pup make the change from indoors to outdoors, take a soiled sheet of newspaper or a used puddle pad that carries the scent of your pup's urine. Put that down in the outdoor elimination area. Place a rock on the paper to prevent a breeze from blowing it away. When it's potty time, leash your pup, take her to the marked outdoor spot, and give the cue you use for elimination. Let your pup stand on that paper when she eliminates outdoors. If your pup sniffs the scented paper, praise her gently and encourage her to do her business. If she starts to

The Litter Box Option

Puppies and small dogs can use a litter box instead of newspapers as an indoor potty place. Training a dog to use a litter box follows the same steps as training her to eliminate outdoors, except instead of taking the pup outside, you'll take her to her litter box.

The Box

Be sure you get a litter box that's wide enough for your dog to turn around in and at least six inches longer than her body. The box should be four to six inches deep. If you can't find a big enough litter box, get a large, shallow, plastic storage box. Save the lid that comes with the storage box. If you decide to teach your dog to ask to use her box, as a dog would ask to go outside, you can train her to scratch the lid of the box as a signal. The lid is also handy to keep the contents of the box from spilling if you take it with you when traveling.

The Litter

There are different types of absorbent materials you can use. The easiest way is simply to line the box with newspaper or a puddle pad. Some

wander away, quietly lead her back to the paper and command her again to go potty.

When your pup has made the connection between potty on paper inside and potty on paper outside, shrink the target area. Each day for four days reduce the size of the paper by half. By the fifth day, leave just a six-inch piece of paper weighted with a rock. The paper won't be big enough for the pup to stand on with all four feet, so she'll potty on the ground. Be sure to praise her warmly, but not excitedly, when she does. (Excited praise can cause a dog to tense up and not be able to finish eliminating.)

The final step in the transition to outdoor elimination is to remove the visual clue (the paper) and replace it with scent only. Do this by taking a paper with the pup's urine on it and pouring water through it onto the ground below. The water will carry the urine scent and mark the spot for your pup.

people tear or shred newspaper to use as litter. Clay or other fine-grain litter made for cats doesn't work too well for most dogs, as it tends to stick to their feet and end up on the floor. A better choice is the pellet type of litter. The pieces are larger and are not as messy as fine-grain litter.

Switching from Papers to the Litter Box

To switch from papers to a litter box, take a section of newspaper or a puddle pad with a bit of your dog's urine on it and place it in the empty litter box. Put the box in the pup's corral where the newspaper area was. When potty time rolls around, place your puppy in the litter box to stand on the familiar paper that has been her elimination surface on the floor. Say her elimination cue to let her know why she's there.

If your puppy hops out of the box before eliminating, calmly lift her back in and give her the elimination cue again. If she sniffs the papers, praise her. If she jumps out again, gently help her back in. Be calm, gentle, and patient or you'll scare your pup and she may never want to use a litter box. If the pup hops out of the box and urinates on the papered floor, don't worry and don't scold. You'll have plenty more chances to teach her how to use the litter box.

The calmer and more matter-of-fact you are, the more readily your pup will accept the litter box. Be patient and persistent; she'll get the idea soon.

Some pups figure out this transition more quickly than others. Some, having stood on a smaller and smaller piece of paper, will go to their spot and eliminate without the paper or scent reminders after just a few days. You may be able to skip some of the steps above if your pup doesn't need the extra help to figure things out.

Establishing a Potty Spot

It's fairly easy to teach a pup to eliminate in only one designated area. Here's how:

- Always take her to the same spot at potty time.
- Don't let her dawdle along the way or she might eliminate somewhere else.
- Always take the pup to visit the potty spot before leaving the yard with her for walks.

It's a big step when your pup realizes there are places to potty and places not to. The puddle pads cover just half of this corral, and the bed in the other half discourages the pups from eliminating anywhere but the pads. Soon they'll be able to make the transition to going outdoors.

When to Switch

Owners of large pups usually switch to outdoors early because of the size of the messes, but newspapers can still be useful if the pup spends a long time in her indoor corral while you're away. Remember, a pup 3 months old needs to eliminate at least every three hours; a 4-month-old at least every four hours. Use the indoor papers as long as your puppy needs them.

Many people use a combination of indoor papers and an outdoor spot. When the pup is confined by herself she can eliminate on the newspaper. When you're available to take her outside, she can do her business in the outdoor spot.

Chapter 7

Outdoor Training

The majority of dog owners train their dogs to eliminate outdoors, even if they start them in the house on newspapers. Many people don't care where their dogs eliminate, as long as they're not soiling in the house. But you can actually be quite specific about where your dog eliminates outdoors. While you're teaching your pup to go outside, you can also teach him to use one particular area.

Selecting an Appropriate Elimination Place

Housetraining will be quicker and easier if you select the right location for your dog's outdoor potty area. An ideal area is one that's flat or gently sloping and less than fifty feet from your door. Pick a spot that's easy to get to day or night and that has enough light so you can see what your dog is doing. Some dogs, especially small ones, don't like getting rained on or buffeted by wind when they're trying to eliminate, so if possible pick an area with a sheltering tree, overhanging deck, or some other protection from the weather.

If you don't have a yard, you could teach your dog to relieve himself in a designated corner of your deck or patio by marking off that area with a "fence" of decorative planters. If you live in an apartment and don't have access to an appropriate grass or dirt area, a square of washable plastic grass-rug on your balcony could be your dog's outdoor elimination spot. If there's no balcony, teach your dog to use the street between two parked cars (and remember to properly dispose of the poop).

Pick a potty spot for your dog that fits your living situation and take him to it consistently.

Safe Confinement

To keep your dog safe when you're not there with him, you'll need to confine him somehow. Chains, ropes, and cable tie-outs are inexpensive but dangerous. They can twist and tangle and sometimes strangle a dog. Free-standing chain-link wire kennel runs are convenient to install, but are lonely and rather cramped for a dog to spend much time in. A kennel run can work as a potty place, but it has its drawbacks. You must take your dog from the house out to his kennel each time he has to eliminate. If it's more than a few steps from your door, you may find yourself tempted to leave your dog out in the kennel too long.

A Fenced Yard Is Best

A fenced yard allows convenient access to and from the house so it doesn't isolate the dog from the rest of the family. Outdoor potty training will be easiest for both of you if your yard can be fenced to include at least one of the doors to your home. After the dog is completely housetrained, you might consider installing a dog door so he can let himself in and out at will.

Country Dogs

Out in the country, we might feel as if we could retreat to the days when dogs could safely run free. Times have changed, though, and roaming free is too dangerous for dogs and is often illegal as well.

If you keep your impressionable young pup from wandering off, he will form the good habit of staying

Even in the country, dogs must be either in a fenced yard or on a leash when they go out.

home. If you just turn your pup loose without guidance, though, he'll find plenty of trouble to get into and may develop the dangerous habit of wandering. Do whatever you must to keep your pup from getting into the roaming habit. Once a dog becomes a vagabond, even a huge acreage won't be big enough to keep him home.

Suburban Dogs

Suburban householders often go to considerable effort and expense to beautify their property. Their understandable pride in home and yard sometimes presents a problem when a dog joins the family. Where can a dog's potty area be located that won't sully the view and spoil the landscaping?

A fenced area for the new dog can be disguised with decorative plants. A fence, hidden by attractive foliage, makes a property more secure without giving it the appearance of a fortress.

Dog Doors

A special door for your dog that opens out into a safely fenced yard, can be a real boon for dogs who must spend long hours alone. Pet doors can be installed in any door or wall, and several styles are available. One type of pet door fits into the opening of a sliding glass door. Pet doors come in a variety of sizes to fit any dog, from a Chihuahua to a Great Dane.

City Dogs

How you housetrain your pup or dog in the city depends on the neighborhood you live in. If you're fortunate, you may have access to a community dog run or a dogs-allowed park where you can exercise and potty your pup. Otherwise, outdoor potty in the big city means your dog will need to learn to eliminate at the curb.

In the city, you absolutely must pick up after your pooch when he defecates. Not only do you owe that courtesy to your neighbors, but cleaning up after your dog benefits dogs and dog owners everywhere. Piles of poop dotting walkways and playgrounds are a major reason cities close their parks to dogs. The best way to counter this is to get rid of the "evidence." Pick up your dog's poop—every time! Even when nobody's watching, even at night, even when the weather is terrible. If every dog owner picked up every time, public parks would be cleaner, and more of them would allow dogs.

Dog Parks

Off-leash dog parks are appearing in more and more cities. Some dog parks are private, with membership dues, identification cards, and gate keys, while others are open to the general public. Dogs play and run and romp while owners watch

If you live in the city, you'll have to take your dog for frequent walks and clean up after him every time.

and chat. When dogs stop playing to do their business, owners stop chatting to do the cleanup. Some dog parks are equipped with plastic bag dispensers or poop scoops, making it easier for owners to comply with pick-up rules.

Training for Outdoor Elimination

To train your dog to eliminate outdoors, leash him and take him to the area you've selected as his potty place. When you first start the training, marking the spot with a scent of the dog's own urine (from newspapers or an "accident") can help make training easier.

Managing Distractions

The world outdoors is a busy and stimulating place. At first your dog may be so interested in everything going on around him that it's hard for him to eliminate. This can make the first few outside potty attempts frustrating for new owners. But be patient and the situation will improve.

Keep him on leash and if he tries to leave, gently stop him and calmly repeat your cue for him to potty. If you give your pup a few minutes in the potty area and he doesn't go, he might not need to yet. If you're keeping track of your dog's daily elimination schedule, you'll know whether this is likely to be the problem. If your dog normally eliminates at this time of day, be patient and wait with him a little longer.

Another reason your dog might not eliminate is that he's too excited to relax the muscles that control elimination. You can solve this problem by standing calmly and occasionally reminding him to do his business. Stay in one place; don't let your pup lead you around looking for the "perfect" spot. You have already shown the dog where to go, now just wait quietly. Your pup will go if he needs to.

When the Pup Won't Eliminate

If you find yourself waiting longer than five minutes for your dog to potty, calmly take him back inside. Watch him carefully for twenty minutes and don't give him any opportunity to slip away to elimi-nate unnoticed. If you're too busy to watch the pup, put him in his

If your pup seems distracted when you take him out, calmly take him back inside and try again later.

crate. After twenty minutes, take him out to the potty spot again and tell him what to do. If he's unsuccessful after five minutes, bring him back in and watch or crate him for fifteen to twenty more minutes. Then give him another chance to eliminate.

Coping with Accidents

When your pup has housetraining accidents—and *all* dogs do—*do not* punish him! It's not his fault; it's yours. You weren't watching closely enough.

Take your pup and a paper towel to the accident. Point to the urine or feces and calmly tell your puppy, "No potty here." Then scoop or sop up the accident with the paper towel and take that and the pup to the approved potty area. Smear the urine or drop the poop on the ground (throw away the paper towel) and tell your dog, "Good potty here," as if he'd done the deed himself in the right place. Praising for elimination in the approved place will help your dog remember the rules.

Chapter 8

Two-Way Communication

Dogs are social creatures, and they communicate clearly with their own kind through body postures and vocal tones. Tones are important in dog communication—no one would mistake a whimper for a growl—but canine stance, facial expressions, and body gestures speak even louder.

Your dog's natural body language can help you train her, if you can interpret body-speak messages. A dog's posture, gestures, and facial expressions convey emotions and needs. Being able to read dog body language will improve your training success.

Previously Kenneled Dogs

Some adolescent or adult dogs who have been kenneled all their lives and have never been in a house may eliminate without a second thought anywhere they happen to be. You will have to watch such a dog very closely because she has no idea that relieving herself in the house is wrong. She needs your help to understand this. Treat this dog as you would a young pup who has never been housetrained. Watch for signs that she needs to relieve herself, give her frequent opportunities to eliminate in the correct area, and go with her so you're there to praise her success.

Some adult kenneled dogs are difficult to housetrain because they're so accustomed to eliminating in their confined area that they no longer care if their den smells of waste. You may have more success in anticipating your dog's needs if you tie her leash to your belt, rather than letting her wander freely in the house. At night, crate her near your own bed, so if she wakes up you'll hear her and be able to take her to her potty area. If you can prevent her from engaging in her old elimination habits for about three months, she'll gradually form new habits and become clean in the house. If you don't work hard at this, though, the dog may soil your house repeatedly and take a much longer time to housetrain.

Why Accidents Happen

Many potty accidents happen because the dog is unable to communicate her needs. When she's feeling the need to eliminate, a pup might rush to the door that leads to her potty area. If that door is closed, the way to success, relief, and praise is blocked. If someone were to let her out at this point, the pup would be happy to eliminate in her designated area. But if no one sees her standing there and opens the door, at some point she won't be able to wait any longer and she'll relieve herself right where she stands.

This isn't the dog's fault. She went to the door intending to go to her potty spot, but the door wouldn't open for her.

If you anticipate your dogs' needs and get them out frequently, housetraining will be a lot easier.

Wandering Off to Eliminate

Instead of going to the door that leads out, a pup or adult who isn't housetrained might head for a remote room of the house. She's looking for a way to get farther from her food and sleeping areas to eliminate, but she might end up using the guest bedroom as her potty area. This is an honest mistake. Many houses are large enough that a dog might think a rarely used room is the equivalent of an indoor backyard.

If you see your dog starting to wander off down the hall, don't assume she's looking for a secluded place to rest. She's more likely looking for a secluded place to eliminate. Keep her with you so you can keep an eye on her body language and know when she needs a potty trip outside.

Teaching Your Dog to Ask to Go Out

There's an easy way to teach a dog to ask to go potty. Your pup can learn to ring a bell with her paw or nose when she wants out.

The Potty Bell

The potty bell should be loud enough that you can hear it from the next room, yet small enough that a pup can easily ring it. A decorative brass bell or a string of sleigh bells works nicely. Hang the bell from the doorknob of the door that leads to the potty area. The bell should hang at about the height of the pup's nose.

Each time you take your dog to her outdoor elimination area, while you're on your way to the door say, "Let's go out, go potty." Ring the bell just before you open the door. After a few dozen times of hearing the bell and then having the door open, the dog will form an association between the two events and start trying out the bell on her own.

You won't have to specifically teach your pup to ring the bell; just ring it yourself. The pup will learn to ring the bell on her own in about a week. Once she makes this connection between the bell ringing and the door opening, she'll have a way to ask to go out when she needs to eliminate.

False Alarms

Once she figures out how to call you to open the door for her, your pup might try using the potty bell when she just wants to go out and play. You can discourage this by escorting your dog directly to the potty area when she rings the bell. Wait with the pup for a reasonable time and don't allow her to play or

It's not difficult to teach your dog to tell you when she needs to go out.

Posture as Language

Understanding your dog's body language can help you win the battle of the puddle. When a dog is ready to eliminate, she'll display a specific set of postures. The sooner you learn to read these signals, the cleaner your floor will be.

When a puppy feels the urge to eliminate, she may start sniffing the ground and circling. These two signals together almost always mean the pup needs to go—and right away. A young pup doesn't get much lag time between the urge and actually eliminating, so you'll need to be quick to intercept her in time. The younger your pup, the more observant you must be.

Defecation Posture

When a puppy is getting ready to defecate, she may run urgently back and forth or in a circle while sniffing the ground. Immediately before defecating, the pup's anus may start to open slightly or protrude. Your pup will squat and hunch her back, with her tail sticking straight out behind. There's no mistaking this posture; nothing else looks like it.

Once your pup takes this position, it's almost too late. So if you want to interrupt her, you'd better hurry! With a young pup, you may have to carry her to the potty area to get there in time.

wander off to explore. Give her a few minutes to get down to business. If she doesn't relieve herself or start showing signs that she needs to, take her back inside. The potty bell is a valuable communication signal, so teach your pup it only works to get to the potty area.

Teaching to Go on Command

There's no "official" command for elimination, so simply choose a word or phrase you feel comfortable saying. Some people use the same word for the pup's elimination as they would for their children. Select a word you won't mind saying in public, because sometimes you'll have to.

Urination Postures

All young puppies, males and females, lower their hindquarters when they urinate, although the posture is slightly different between the sexes. Females look almost like they're sitting. Males don't squat that low, but stretch out a little and spread their hind legs.

If your pup is under 4 months, the beginning of that squat is your cue to hurry her to the potty area. Pups under 3 months have very little time to get to the right spot once they feel the urge to urinate. From 3 to 6 months, they can hold their urine a few seconds longer between the urge and the act.

Leg Lifting

Most adult female dogs squat to urinate, although some manage to lift one hind leg while squatting. Adult males usually lift a rear leg when urinating, which enables them to mark territory more efficiently by aiming the stream against an upright object. Some will mark an object and then turn around, hike up the other leg, and mark it again.

Male pups may not cock a leg to urinate until they reach adolescence at about 6 months. An occasional precocious male might start lifting his leg as young as 2 to 3 months. Male pups usually first start lifting a leg to pee after watching a more mature dog urinate that way. Once the leg-lifting habit is in place, male dogs seldom revert to squatting to urinate.

When you take your dog to eliminate, say the cue word. When she produces, praise her softly using the cue word in a praise phrase: "good go potty."

Caught in the Act

If you see your pup about to relieve herself somewhere other than the designated area, interrupt her immediately. Say "wait, wait, wait!" to gently startle her into stopping. Then praise the pup and carry her or lead and encourage her to the correct area. Once she's in the potty area, give her the cue to eliminate. Use a friendly voice for the cue, then wait patiently for her to produce.

The pup may be tense because you just startled her, and she may need to relax a little before she's able to go. When she does her job, include the cue in the praise: "good go potty."

Teaching your dog to eliminate on command will make both your lives a lot easier.

Finding Accidents After the Fact

Urine and feces carry a dog's unique scent, which she (and every other dog) can instantly recognize. When they smell their own urine or feces, dogs know it's theirs. So if you happen upon a potty mistake after the fact, you can use this to help your dog learn.

When you find a fresh potty mistake, calmly take a paper towel and your dog to the scene of the accident. Point to the evidence and tell your dog, "no potty here!" Then, using the paper towel, pick up the pile or sop up some of the puddle and take that and your dog to the proper elimination spot. Drop the poop or smear the pee on the ground (hide the paper towel or it will distract your pup) and give your dog her cue to eliminate.

She may not need to go again yet, but wait there with her for a few minutes. If your pup sniffs the evidence, praise her ("good potty!") as if she'd done it there herself. If she eliminates, praise her warmly. Afterward, go finish cleaning up the mess and resolve to watch her more closely to prevent future mistakes.

Should Your Pup See You Clean Up?

Some people say you should never let a pup see you clean up her messes. Others say you should make her watch. So what should you do? Actually, it really doesn't seem to make a difference, so just do what's convenient.

Some pups get excited by the cleaning motions of the mop or paper towels and try to chase and pounce on them. If your pup might do this, it's better to

Take your dog's fresh potty mistake outside and calmly show her where it belongs.

close her away from that area while you're cleaning it. Otherwise, in the excitement of the "game" she may lose the meaning of the lesson.

What About Punishment?

The old-fashioned way of housetraining involved punishing a dog's mistakes even before she understood what she was supposed to do. Puppies were punished for breaking rules they didn't know concerning functions they couldn't control. This was terribly unfair.

Don't Punish Errors

Help your puppy get to the potty place on time. Praise her success when she produces. Do not punish elimination errors. It doesn't do any good to punish a pup for a behavior she isn't yet able to control. As your dog matures and gains control of body functions, she will take herself to the potty place when she needs to go. Until then, take the time to teach your pup where you want her to eliminate.

Spanking, hitting, shaking, or scaring a puppy for having a housetraining accident is confusing and counterproductive. A pup isn't likely to make any connection between the punishment and having relieved herself. Instead, spend your energy on positive forms of teaching. Your dog will learn faster if you help her succeed than if you hurt or frighten her for making mistakes.

There's no need or reason to punish your dog to housetrain her. It's your job to take your dog to the potty area before she needs to go, especially with pups under 3 months. If you aren't watching your pup closely enough and she has an accident, don't punish the puppy. It wasn't her fault; it was yours.

Chapter 9

A Schedule Will Help

What goes in must come out." While that's a somewhat oversimplified description of digestion and elimination, it is nonetheless accurate. When and what your pup eats, and when it is digested, controls the timing of his elimination needs. Regulating his access to food will therefore make his elimination needs more predictable

Water intake and urination work in much the same way, but pups need to drink frequently to stay healthy, so water intake should not be limited—except during the night. Allow your pup free access to fresh water all day. Water consumption is highest right after eating, so feeding your pup meals at regular intervals will help regulate the timing of both urine and feces.

This clear relationship between intake and output is good news for anyone housetraining a puppy. Controlling when, what, and how much your pup eats will help you predict when he needs to go outside. Housetraining a pup under 12 weeks of age is largely a matter of getting him to the potty spot at the right time. Knowing in advance when the "right time" will occur will save you a lot of cleanups and fruitless trips to the potty area.

Of course, if you want to predict when the poop comes out, you will have to be predictable about when the food goes in. If you leave food available for your dog to snack on all day, it will throw off the predictability of his potty needs. A regular feeding and exercise schedule can help your pup learn to be clean, and it can even fix some difficult and resistant housetraining problems in adolescent and adult dogs.

Scheduling Basics

The timing of feeding, sleep, play, and potty will change depending on the age of your dog. Young puppy bodies require more frequent filling and emptying than older pups and adults.

With a new puppy in your home, don't be surprised if your rising time is suddenly a bit earlier than you're used to. Puppies tend to be early risers, and when your pup awakens at the crack of dawn you'll have to get up and take him to his elimination area. This may disrupt your sleep pattern for a few weeks, but be patient. In just a few months he may enjoy sleeping in as much as you do.

It's fine to adjust rising times when you're using the schedules in this chapter, but don't adjust the intervals between feedings and potty outings unless your pup's behavior justifies the change. The intervals between meals and potty times are more important than what hour your day begins. Your puppy can only meet your expectations in housetraining if you keep your goals age-appropriate for him.

Use these schedules as a basic plan or template to help prevent potty accidents. Meanwhile, use your powers of observation to discover how best to modify the basic schedule to fit your dog's own unique needs. Each dog is an individual and will have his own body rhythms.

If you schedule what goes into your dog, you will also be able to predict when it comes out.

Home Alone

The schedules for puppies are devised under the assumption that someone will be home most of the time with the pup. That would be best, of course, but it's not always possible. If you must leave your pup alone during his early housetraining period, be sure to cover the entire floor of his playpen or puppy corral with puddle pads or thick layers of newspaper. If you come home to messes in the puppy's daytime area, don't make a big deal about it, just clean it up. If you were able to be

Crate Abuse

Do not use your pup's sleeping crate to store him while you go off to work for eight hours. A puppy needs to move around and exercise. He needs to play, eat, and drink. And he'll definitely need to eliminate. Your pup can't do all that in a crate. It's just too small a space. He needs a playpen or puppy corral. Crating a pup for the whole day is unfair and unhealthy. Don't do it.

home, your pup would have someone to remind him where to go potty. Be patient—he's just a baby.

You can ease the problems of a latchkey pup by having a neighbor or friend look in on the dog at noon and take him to eliminate. Another solution might be hiring a pet sitter to drop by at midday. A professional pet sitter will be knowledgeable about dogs and able to give your pup high-quality care and socialization. Some will even help train your pup in both potty manners and basic obedience. Unlike a neighbor or friend, a professional pet sitter won't get annoyed or bored taking care of your pup every day. Ask your veterinarian and your dog-owning friends to recommend a good pet sitter.

Puppies need to eliminate after play and exercise.

Schedule for Pups Under 10 Weeks

If your work schedule is such that you can't be with your puppy during the day, realize that housetraining may progress more slowly than if you were there to coach him.

11:00 p.m.	Lay out easy-on clothes and shoes before going to bed. There will be no time to choose your wardrobe in the morning when you jump out of bed to take your pup to his potty place. And don't forget your house keys!
7:00 a.m.	Get up and take the puppy from his sleeping crate directly to the potty spot. Carry him if necessary.
7:15	Clean up last night's messes, if any.
7:30	Feed and water the pup.
7:45	Pick up the food bowl. Take the pup to his potty spot; wait and praise.
8:00	The pup plays around your feet while you drink coffee and prepare breakfast. It has now been one hour since you got up. Console yourself that, if you've been following this schedule so far, you shouldn't have had any new messes to clean up for the past hour.
8:15	Potty time again.
8:30	Put the pup in his crate for a nap.
10:00	When the pup wakes, out to potty.
10:15	The puppy is in his corral with safe toys to chew and play with. As you watch your pup at play, observe his behavior. Learn to recognize what he does immediately before eliminating. Any sudden searching, sniffing, or circling behavior is a likely sign he has to go. As soon as you see that, carry or lead the pup to his potty spot and calmly tell him to eliminate. Praise his success. If you miss the moment and arrive some time after the flood, do not scold or punish. It's not the pup's fault you were late.

10:45	Potty break.
11:00	Play time.
11:30	Potty time again.
11:45	Food and fresh water.
12:00 p.m.	Pick up the food bowl and take the pup to his potty spot.
12:15	Crate the pup for a nap with a safe chew toy.
2:00	Potty break.
2:15	Snack and beginner obedience training practice.
2:45	Potty break.
3:00	Put the pup in his corral with safe toys and chews for solitary play and/or a nap.
4:15	Potty break.
4:30	Make the pup a part of household activities by putting him on a leash and taking him around the house with you. Watch and guide your pup's behavior. When he needs to eliminate, you'll be right there to notice, take him to the right spot in time, and praise his good job.
5:00	Food and fresh water.
5:15	Potty break.
5:30	The pup may play nearby (either leashed or in his corral) while you prepare your evening meal.
6:00	Potty break, then crate the pup while you eat and clean up after dinner.
7:00	Potty break.
7:15	Leashed or closely watched, this is a good time for the pup to play and socialize with family and visitors for a few hours. Offer the pup water occasionally throughout the evening (a dog needs water to digest his food). Take the pup to his potty spot whenever he acts like he needs to go.
9:00	Last water of the evening.

(continued)

(continued)

9:15	Potty break. Then crate the pup or keep him close to you. Do not let him wander off unescorted.
10:45	Last chance to potty.
11:00	Put the pup to bed in his crate for the night. Go to bed yourself and get some rest. You've earned it!
3:00 or 4:00 a.m.	Your pup awakes and has to eliminate. Take him to the potty spot and make sure he does everything he has to do. Then re-crate the pup with a safe, quiet chew toy and go back to sleep.

Keep your puppy with you as much as possible to teach him about the world around him.

Schedule for Pups 10 Weeks to 6 Months

As your pup grows from 10 weeks to 6 months, he'll require progressively less frequent feeding and potty visits but more play and social time. During this period, keep your puppy with you as much as possible. He needs to learn about all the amazing things in his world. The pup will learn to look to you for guidance and follow your lead during this period. Give him good opportunities to do this by tying his leash to your belt when you're busy around the house. Not only will you be right there to prevent potty accidents, but you'll also be available to guide your pup's behavior around people, property, and any other pets you have.

7:00 a.m.	Get up and take the puppy from his sleeping crate to his potty spot.
7:15	Clean up last night's messes, if any.
7:30	Feed and water the pup.
7:45	Pick up the food bowl. Take the pup to his potty spot; wait and praise.
8:00	The pup plays around your feet while you have your breakfast.
9:00	Potty break.
9:15	Play and obedience practice.
10:00	Potty break.
10:15	The puppy is in his corral with safe toys to chew and play with.
11:30	Potty break.
11:45	Food and fresh water.
12:00 p.m.	Pick up the food bowl and take the pup to his potty spot.
12:15	The puppy is in his corral with safe toys to chew and play with.
1:00	Potty break.
1:15	Put the pup on a leash and take him around the house with you.
3:30	Potty break.
3:45	Put the pup in his corral with safe toys and chews for solitary play and/or a nap.
4:45	Potty break.
5:00	Food and fresh water.
5:15	Potty break.
5:30	The pup may play nearby (either leashed or in his corral) while you prepare your evening meal.
7:00	Potty break.
7:15	Leashed or closely watched, the pup may play and socialize with family and visitors.
9:15	Potty break.
10:45	Last chance to potty.
11:00	Put the pup to bed in his crate for the night.

> ## Meals Versus Free Feeding
>
> Although many owners allow their adolescent and adult dogs to free feed, this is not appropriate if you're trying to house-train. Regular meals mean regular elimination for dogs of any age. Some adult dogs do quite well on one meal a day, but most professionals recommend feeding all dogs twice a day.

Schedule for Adolescent and Adult Dogs

An older pup or adult dog who isn't yet housetrained must be watched and regulated as closely as a young pup. He may not have to eliminate as often as a baby pup, but an adolescent or adult dog who hasn't been fully housetrained might relieve himself wherever he happens to be when the urge strikes. As you learn your dog's habits and rhythms, it will be increasingly easy to anticipate his needs.

7:00 a.m.	Get up and take the dog from his sleeping crate directly to the potty spot.
7:30	Food and fresh water.
7:45	Pick up the food bowl and take the dog to his potty spot.
8:00	Allow the dog to play or lounge with you. Provide chew toys.
10:00	Potty break.
10:15	Play and obedience practice.
11:45	Potty break.
12:00 p.m.	Food and fresh water.
12:15	Pick up the food bowl and take the dog to his potty spot.
12:45	Solitary play in the room with you or outdoors in a fenced yard.

2:45	Potty break.
3:00	Put the dog on a leash and take him around the house with you. If he is reliably house-trained, this can be free time.
5:00	Food and fresh water.
5:15	Pick up the food bowl and take the dog to his potty spot.
5:30	Keep the dog with you while you prepare and eat your meal.
7:15	Potty break.
7:30	Closely watched, the dog plays off leash and socializes with the family.
9:30	Potty break.
10:45	Last chance to potty.
11:00	Crate the dog for the night.

Adult dogs still need to be walked several times a day. Even if you have a fenced yard where the dog can eliminate, daily walks exercise the dog's mind and body.

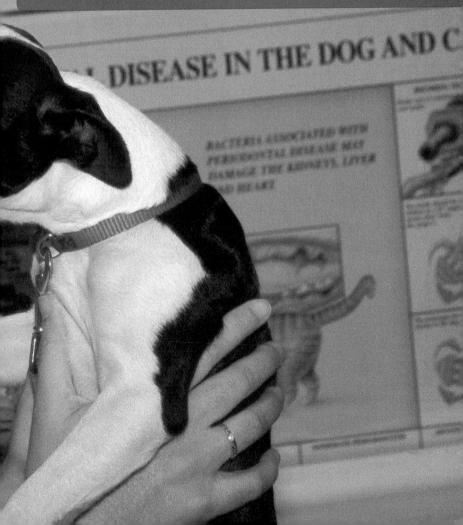

Part III

Special Housetraining Problems

Chapter 10

Recurring Elimination Problems

S ome elimination problems can occur repeatedly, despite your attempts to convince your dog to use the designated potty area. Instead of giving in to frustration and anger, try to figure out why your dog is having trouble complying with your wishes. Persistent potty mistakes often stem from ages-old instinctive canine behavior.

Marking

Lately "dominance" has become a catchword to explain almost every undesirable canine behavior, but it's really not an indication the dog is an evil genius trying to take over the world. Dominance is more the canine equivalent of natural high self-esteem. In a wild dog pack, the leader must be strong and decisive to prevent arguments within the group and keep everyone safe from outside attack. One thing the boss dog does to keep outsiders away is use urine and feces to mark the pack's turf.

A dog's urine and feces carry his unique scent, and when they are deposited on an object or territory, they mark that property as the dog's own. When a dog wants to mark his trail or territory, he urinates.

A dominant dog will normally claim as much real estate as he can. This becomes a problem if he starts claiming his owner's belongings as his own. It happens most often with dogs who are alone more than they're with the family. Try to imagine this situation from the dog's point of view. You're not home as much as the dog is, so it's really the dog's turf, not yours. You just sleep there at night and maybe hang around on weekends. If the home-alone dog marks property while you're gone, he may believe he's marking his own territory, not yours.

TIP

Marking behavior is more frequently seen in male dogs, but some females may also mark.

You come home and wash it off. He marks it again the next day. You wash it off again. He marks again. You may start feeling as if you're at war with your dog, but all he's doing is renewing his scent mark to protect "his" territory from outsiders.

This perfectly natural canine behavior can be very messy and destructive for you. It's hard to keep from being frustrated and angry with a dog who urinates on your stuff. Obviously, marking must be controlled if you share your home with the dog.

Managing Marking

A dog who marks must be given plenty of outdoor exercise. At least some of this exercise should be on a leash, so you're able to direct the dog to mark appropriate objects, such as rocks and trees. He needs to learn to mark only where you approve.

A dog marks to claim territory as his own.

Teach him a cue to mark. When you take him to a good marking spot, such as a hydrant or a clump of tall grass, give him enough slack on the leash so he can sniff freely there and tell him "mark it." If he pees there, praise him, "good mark it!" If he goes toward other areas to sniff and pee, gently pull him away, saying "no mark." Then take him to a different spot where it's okay for him to pee and cue him, "mark it." Praise when he does. By placing marking on cue and choosing where you allow it, your dog will begin to realize he can't just pee on anything he happens to feel like marking.

Some dogs who mark do so more when they're bored and underexercised. Ask a friend or hire a professional pet sitter to walk your dog once or twice a day while you're at work. Your dog will get needed exercise, have opportunities to eliminate in approved areas, and be less bored than if he were just waiting at home for you. Bored dogs have nothing better to do than chew, bark, mark, and mess while you're gone. Less time spent alone can have a positive effect on a dog's behavior and attitude.

Find interesting activities to share with your dog when you are home. Watching TV reruns together is not enough. Find something more active to do. Go for walks in new places, play games, teach tricks, or take an obedience or agility class together. Exercising your dog's mind and muscles every day will improve your dog-owner relationship and is one of the best ways to decrease behavior problems of all types.

To manage marking, introduce your dog to acceptable marking spots, such as trees, and teach him a cue that tells him it's okay to mark there.

Doggie Diapers

If closer confinement while your dog is indoors doesn't stop the marking problem, or if marking occurs even when you're home, you can put diapers on your dog. No kidding! Not baby diapers, but special waterproof absorbent garments made for dogs. There are belly bands for males and doggie panties for females. These garments come in all sizes, so any dog can be fit with them. Inside the garment is a pocket that holds an absorbent pad that catches the urine and keeps it off the floor, walls, and furniture. These garments are available at pet supply stores and through catalogs and the Internet.

Wearing the garment keeps dogs from being able to mark, so scent spots don't get continually reanointed and renewed. Also, instead of the urine hitting the intended target, the dog ends up "wearing" it. (Be sure to change the pad as soon as it gets wet, so the urine won't irritate the dog's skin.) This is enough reason for some dogs to stop marking in the house, but others—most often toy breed males—will continue to try. These dogs may need to wear their garment in the house for quite some time before they fully give up the habit. You can determine their progress by checking the pad for wetness.

Submissive Urination

Submissive urination can be viewed as the opposite of marking. The dog urinates not because she's trying to be the boss, but because she's knows she's not. Submissive urination is sometimes seen in males but is more common in immature females. Some keep their piddling habit into adulthood, but it usually isn't as extreme as in puppyhood.

In some young dogs, the urethral valves are not sufficiently developed to hold back urine when the dogs are excited. Maturity will alleviate the problem. True submissive urination is an expression of respect, not a problem with underdeveloped valves.

Greet a submissive piddler outdoors.

If a dog piddles at your feet when she says hello, when you bend or reach over her, or when you scold her, that dog is urinating submissively. She does this to let you know you are her hero and that nothing could make her turn against you. Try to feel flattered by this soggy display, instead of upset. The dog doesn't intend to anger you; she's just trying to show you she's nothing but a wet-bottomed dog with no desire to be your rival.

Managing Submissive Urination

You cannot discourage submissive urination by punishing or scolding. If you respond angrily the dog will simply try harder to convince you of her submission, and she can only do that by peeing more. You could drown before you stop a submissive piddler by punishing her.

The best way to manage submissive urination is to keep everything low-key. Don't look at, talk to, or bend to pet your dog when she's excited. If she tends to pee when you greet her, keep homecomings calm. It often works best not to greet the dog or even acknowledge her until you've been home for five minutes or so and she's had a chance to calm down.

Greet the submissive piddler outdoors, if possible. Then if she wets, it's not a problem. Walk around as you greet the dog rather than stopping to pet her. Speak quietly and avoid high-pitched talk. The more mellow the greeting, the less likely your dog will be to piddle when she sees you.

Hiding Elimination

Some owners punish their dogs for potty accidents, and this is a big mistake. Punishment can scare a dog and cause her to fear her owner's anger, while not helping her to understand exactly what the anger is about. If the dog figures out that your wrath had something to do with eliminating, she may do her best never to let you see her eliminate.

This can create several problems. Not realizing there is a right place to eliminate, the dog may think the owner wants her never to eliminate at all. A dog with that idea will refuse to eliminate in front of her owner, so escorted trips to the elimination area will bear no fruit. Because this dog cannot eliminate while the owner is present, she must wait until she can be alone. This dog will sneak off to leave puddles and messes behind furniture or in little-used rooms of the house.

At first, the owner may not realize this behavior is happening because the dog is careful to do it only when there's nobody watching. The odor may be noticeable, but no evidence will be in view. Only when a guest arrives to use the extra bedroom or when the furniture is rearranged will the hidden deeds be discovered. The rug in the spare room or behind the sofa will be spotted like a Dalmatian, and there may be weeks' worth of petrified poop. Upon discovering the crime scene, some owners fly into a rage and severely punish the dog. Others simply sigh and hope for better behavior in the future. Neither of these reactions will help change the dog's habit.

Correcting the Hiding

If your dog has been hiding her elimination from you, there's a reason for it. Your dog is trying her best not to give you any cause to be angry about her elimination. If she knew a way to please you with appropriate potty behavior, she would have no reason to hide her output.

If you punish your dog for accidents, she may look for a secret spot in the house to eliminate. Instead, calmly clean up after your dog and remember she is just a baby.

Is It Spite?

Dogs aren't generally a spiteful lot, so when owners assume spite is the motive for unacceptable elimination, they're usually mistaken. The dog isn't trying to "get back at you" for leaving her there alone. She has a different reason doing for what she's done.

What is often viewed as "spite elimination" usually occurs while the owner is away and the dog is alone in the house. In a typical scenario, the dog has been reliably housetrained and has been given the run of the home, with no potty accidents for some time. The owner returns home from work one day to find urine or feces on the bed or couch. The owner scolds the dog and thoroughly cleans the soiled spots. But then the same thing happens the next day and again a few days later. Spite? Not likely. You'll need to look for a different cause.

To cure potty-hiding behavior, you'll need to convince your dog there is a praiseworthy place to eliminate. The best way to do this is to start over again with housetraining, as if you had just brought the dog home.

First and foremost, if you have been punishing the dog for elimination mistakes, stop immediately. Your dog probably doesn't understand the rules you're trying to enforce, so she doesn't know she's breaking them. You'll only confuse and frighten her with punishment, and this will delay learning and increase frustration for both you and the dog.

When you're home and can watch your dog closely, you could allow her to be free in the room with you. But if you're too involved in something else to watch the dog every second, tie her leash to your belt and let her follow you like a shadow. If she tries to sneak off, the leash will prevent that and you'll be able to notice when the dog needs to relieve herself.

Tell the dog in a friendly voice that it's time to go to her elimination place, then take her there and wait for her to go. Turn your back so she has some privacy, but keep her in the corner of your vision. When she eliminates, praise her very calmly and admire her puddle or pile. Stay in the potty area for few more minutes after the dog has finished, occasionally giving more calm praise. This will let her know you're not upset with her when she eliminates and will help her realize there is a proper place for it.

Don't scoop the poop right then or the dog may think you really don't approve after all. Let the poop remain where it is until after the dog has been put to bed that night. (Unless, of course, the spot is not on your property; then you must pick it all up.) Then clean up all but a tiny bit, leaving just a little "reminder" to scent the spot for the next day.

Toy Breeds

Many toy breed dogs have persistent troubles with housetraining. Each time a dog eliminates in an approved area, the good habit of doing so is fortified. Each time a dog eliminates in the wrong place, a bad habit is strengthened. Toy dogs are not any dirtier or more stubborn than their larger cousins, but because of their small size it's easier for elimination mistakes to go undiscovered until the behavior has been going on for some time.

With toy breeds, the accidental (or intentional) puddle may consist of only a few teaspoons of urine. This tiny amount may evaporate or disappear into the carpet before it can be discovered. Owners may have no idea their dog has been peeing all over the house until the place begins to reek of urine. Each time a dog eliminates in the wrong place, the habit becomes stronger and harder to change.

Owners must be watchful to catch the dog before she urinates and take her to her elimination area. When the scent of her urine and feces is detectable only in her designated potty place, the dog will realize that's the place to go. However, if the smell of elimination is scattered around in many areas, the dog will not remember which spot is the right one.

Addressing the Needs of Toy Breeds

The best solution is to limit the area the dog is allowed to freely roam. A baby gate will keep the little piddler in the same room with you, so you can maintain a close watch. Or you might tie the dog's leash to your belt so she has no choice but to stay right with you. That way you won't miss her body signals when she needs to eliminate.

For a minimum of three weeks, you must prevent your dog from

Toy breeds may have persistent housetraining problems, simply because their mistakes are harder to find.

making her habitual mistakes. It will take at least that long for the dog to form the new habit of eliminating in the appropriate area. When you can't watch your dog closely, either crate her or confine her to her puppy corral with newspapers on the floor.

Everything about toy dogs is in miniature except their intellect and determination. Little dogs are very bright, but can cling to bad habits as stubbornly as a giant. Repetition of appropriate elimination behavior and praise for success are the keys to ending a toy dog's potty accidents.

Mounting

Mounting is a male sexual posture, but it's also a pushy play behavior in both males and females—even those who have been neutered. A dog may mount objects such as pillows or stuffed toys, other dogs, or even humans.

Sometimes a urethral infection or other irritation of the urinary tract can cause excessive mounting. A dog with a urinary health problem may feel pain or itching that is temporarily relieved when he mounts and rubs himself.

Managing Mounting

When mounting is caused by an infection or irritation, the cure is medical intervention. If your dog mounts often, take him to the veterinarian to be checked for urinary tract problems. You won't be able to stop this behavior simply through training if it's caused by a health problem.

Urinary tract infections and irritations can be cured with swift and proper treatment. Once firmly entrenched, however, infections can be difficult to eradicate and may cause permanent kidney damage. If your dog is mounting and rubbing, get his health checked right away.

Chapter 11

Health-Related Problems

Not all elimination problems are behavior problems. There are a number of health-related reasons a dog might be unable to maintain his house-training. Some of these problems are inherited, some are infectious, and some are caused by environmental factors.

If a dog eliminates inappropriately because he's ill, obviously the solution is to have him treated by a veterinarian. However, it isn't always easy to tell when a dog is unwell. If your housetrained adult suddenly starts urinating in the house, have him checked for health problems immediately.

Many health-related elimination problems can be helped or cured with proper care. Delaying medical treatment can cause great suffering and possibly result in the dog's death. If your dog is having problems controlling his bowels or bladder, before you assume that he's soiling deliberately, take him to the veterinarian for a thorough health check.

How the Elimination System Works

Dog owners sometimes become frustrated with persistent housetraining problems and punish the dog without realizing the trouble has a physical cause. It's unfair to blame a dog for potty accidents he can't control. Being aware of how your dog's body works will help you avoid misunderstandings.

A dog's elimination system is closely integrated with his digestive and reproductive systems. A disease or abnormality in any of these three systems can cause or worsen problems in the other two. When the dog consumes food and liquids, they are processed by the digestive system and the nutrients are sent around the body by the bloodstream. The wastes are then moved out of the body via intestinal and urinary elimination. Both male and female bodies digest food and eliminate solid waste the same way, but anatomical differences between the sexes influence the workings of their urinary systems.

Urinary System

A normal dog of either sex has two kidneys. The kidneys filter metabolic toxins from the dog's body and excrete them in the urine. The ureters transport urine from the kidneys to the bladder, where it is held until it passes through the urethra during urination.

In male dogs the outside opening of the urethra is at the tip of the penis. The male's urethra is relatively long and narrow. The prostate gland surrounds the urethra at the base of the bladder.

The female's urethra is shorter but wider than the male's. The urethra exits the female's body through the vaginal opening. There is no prostate gland.

Some urinary problems affect both sexes, while others are common in one gender but not the other. Neutering can affect both male and female urinary conditions if the causes are hormonal.

Urinary tract problems can affect dogs of either sex and at any age.

Urinary Incontinence

Voluntary urination involves muscles in the bladder wall, valves in the urethra, and abdominal pressure. Urinary incontinence is the inability to voluntarily control one or several of these parts.

A number of health problems can cause excessive or uncontrollable urination. If your pup or dog seems to pee a lot, or if he's over 4 months old and still isn't catching on to housetraining, have your veterinarian check for health-related causes.

Do not delay this health check. Urination problems are not only messy and annoying, they can become life threatening. Kidney damage can result from relatively minor infections. When kidneys are

If your pup or dog seems to urinate a lot, or if he's over 4 months old and still isn't catching on to housetraining, have your veterinarian check for health-related causes.

damaged they may shut down, causing toxins to build up to dangerous levels. Untreated urinary tract infections can also travel through the bloodstream and settle into the spine.

Structurally Based Incontinence

The urethral valves normally prevent leakage between urinations. Incomplete or weak urethral valves are one cause of incontinence. A nerve that is pinched between vertebrae can be another cause. Males can become incontinent if they have prostate problems, but incontinence is much more common in females.

Most at risk are medium to large females. Some have an abnormally positioned bladder with a shorter than normal urethra. Others have a structural abnormality that allows urine to pool in the vagina.

Hormonally Based Incontinence

By far the most common cause of urinary incontinence in females is a low blood level of the hormone estrogen. Ninety percent of females with urinary incontinence have been spayed, and half of those develop the problem within one year after spaying. Some researchers warn against early spaying for this reason, but even when dogs are spayed after maturity, estrogen-related urinary incontinence can develop.

Symptoms of Urinary Incontinence

Urinary incontinence does not manifest in the same way in every dog who has it. The dog may void urine without being aware he has done so. This can happen while he's awake or asleep. In some, there is a continuous dribbling of urine. In others, the escape of urine is intermittent and related to a rise in pressure inside the bladder, as when the dog coughs or sneezes, jumps, lies down, or becomes excited.

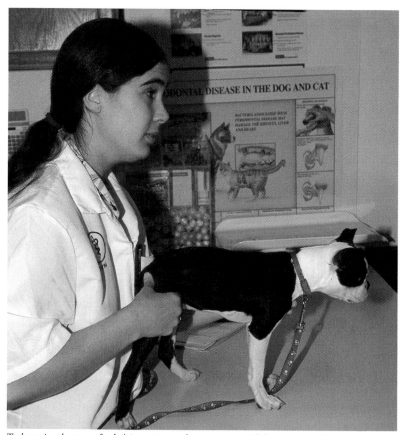

To determine the cause of a dog's incontinence, the veterinarian will do a complete physical exam.

Giving Medicine to Your Dog

It's easy to medicate a dog if you know how.

Liquid Medicine. Check first to find out if your dog likes the taste. Put a drop on the end of your finger and offer it to your dog. If he licks it off, try a second drop. If the dog will lick medicine off your finger twice, he will probably lap up the dosage from a bowl.

If your dog doesn't like the flavor, you'll have to use Plan B. Put the dose in a spoon or a needle-less syringe (ask your veterinarian for one). Pull out the corner of the dog's lip to form a pocket and pour the medicine into it. Then immediately tilt the dog's head up, gently holding his mouth closed, and lightly stroke his throat until he swallows.

Pills. If your dog has any appetite, you may be able to slip him a pill hidden in some tasty food. Processed cheese works well, or any food your dog will gulp greedily that's sticky enough to hold a pill until it's been swallowed. Be sure to ask your veterinarian if the medicine can be given with food.

If your dog tends to lick off the food and then spit out the pill, try this trick: Prepare three identical bits of food and put the pill in one. Give the dog a piece without the pill, so he can discover there's no hidden "agenda." When he finishes that piece, give him the one with the pill. Then, as soon as it's in his mouth, quickly offer him the third piece. Most dogs will instantly swallow the food bit with the pill and greedily grab the final piece.

If a pup seems very difficult to housetrain, or a dog who has been trained for some time starts having urine accidents, he may need veterinary attention. A great wrong is done when owners, frustrated by a dog's uncontrolled urination, punish the dog for breaking housetraining. Before you get angry with your dog about uncontrolled peeing, take him to the doctor to rule out physical problems. A dog with a physical cause for incontinence may be helped through proper medication, but punishment will not help at all.

Treatment and Aftercare

To determine the cause of a dog's incontinence, the veterinarian will do a complete physical exam. This may include genital and rectal examinations, urinalysis and urine culture, and X-rays or ultrasound. Once the cause has been identified, treatment can begin.

If the incontinence is caused by an abnormally positioned bladder, the veterinarian will surgically correct it. Hormonal imbalance in females will be treated with estrogen or other drugs. Medication may also be prescribed to improve the urethral seal.

Home care involves administering the prescribed medication. If the dog does not respond to medication or surgery, care involves keeping her clean, dry, and as comfortable as possible. Trim the hair short around the genital area so urine evaporates quickly and doesn't burn the dog's skin. Petroleum jelly smeared over the genital area will further protect from the irritation of constant wetness.

Incontinence While Asleep

A dog who urinates in his sleep will need special care for his bedding. It must be kept clean and dry, or the dog's skin will be irritated and both the dog and the bedding will smell terrible. A synthetic fleece pad atop newspapers or puddle pads makes a good washable bed for an incontinent dog. Urine can seep through the fleece into the absorbent material below, so the dog remains as dry as possible. Another solution is a fabric cot-type bed that allows urine to drain through instead of being absorbed. A sheet of plastic under the dog's bed will protect the floor.

Cystitis and Urinary Tract Infections

Cystitis is an inflammation of the lining of the bladder. The usual cause is infection by bacteria that enter through the urethra. Cystitis is more common in females than in males because the female urethra provides a shorter, easier path for bacteria to enter the bladder.

In both sexes, the urethra normally has some bacteria in it from outside contamination. If everything functions properly, the bacteria are washed away by urine when the bladder is emptied. It's important that urination occurs frequently enough to keep bacteria flushed out, or else they will migrate up the urethra and enter the bladder. Once inside the bladder, bacteria cause infection and inflammation of the bladder lining. An infection of the bladder can lead to severe kidney disease if it is not successfully treated.

The Importance of Water

All living creatures need water to survive. A dog needs water to digest food and excrete wastes, and to prevent dehydration, low blood pressure, and life-threatening shock. You should allow your dog free access to fresh water so that he can drink as much as he wants.

Strictly limiting water intake was once thought to be a valid way to control a dog's need to urinate. We now know this is a dangerously unhealthy idea. Without sufficient water, a dog may develop cystitis, which makes housetraining nearly impossible because it disrupts the voluntary control of urination. Free access to water can prevent and help cure several conditions that cause uncontrolled urination. Plenty of water and ample opportunities to urinate will keep your dog healthy and speed up housetraining.

Anything that causes a dog to urinate less frequently than normal can put him at risk for developing cystitis. Two common causes of cystitis are insufficient drinking water and insufficient opportunity to urinate, both of which are under your control.

Symptoms of Cystitis

If your dog voids small amounts of urine at frequent intervals, he may have cystitis. This is not the same as marking behavior in which urine is voluntarily "rationed" in small quantities. A dog with cystitis will experience discomfort when urinating. Males who normally lift a leg to pee may squat instead. Females may squat in the normal position but remain there longer and not void as much urine as they normally do. There may be a tinge of blood in the urine and the dog may have a painful and sensitive abdomen.

For a dog with this condition, urination can be very painful, so the dog tries to hold back as long as possible. Finally, he can't help but urinate, so he seeks a place of comfort in his misery. He may pee in his crate or on his bed. Or he may go into your bedroom and urinate on your bed, hoping his special person's special bed will protect him from pain.

To prevent cystitis, make sure your dog always has plenty of fresh water to drink.

A dog who seeks comfort from pain during urination by going on his owner's bed usually has a strong positive attachment to that person. This behavior often shocks and distresses owners, and some jump to the conclusion that the dog is soiling willfully. Some owners will punish the unfortunate dog instead of seeking the medical care he needs.

Treatment and Aftercare

Cystitis is a painful condition, but it usually responds quickly to treatment if it is caught early. In the early stages, a bladder infection usually clears up quickly with a round of antibiotics. Persistent infections may require longer treatment.

To prevent or recover from this condition, a dog needs plenty of fluid intake and output. A dog recovering from cystitis should be encouraged to drink plenty of water. Change the dog's drinking water several times a day to keep it fresh and appetizing. That alone will encourage most dogs to drink more.

Give your dog frequent opportunities to urinate. Don't force him to hold his urine all day while he waits for you to come home. When you're not there to let him out to relieve himself, give him access to a safely fenced area through a pet door, or train him to go indoors on newspapers or in a litter box. Holding his urine for long periods can cause cystitis all by itself.

Urolithiasis

Uroliths are mineral stones that can form in the urinary system. Most uroliths are made of struvite (magnesium ammonium phosphate). Others contain cystine, urate, or oxalate as the main ingredient. Different types of uroliths are treated with different medications and procedures, but all can cause pain and problems with urination.

They are most often found in the bladder, but may migrate into the urethra and, if they are too large to pass, become lodged there. In serious cases, uroliths can completely block the urethra, preventing urine from passing. This can lead to sudden kidney failure and death.

A dog of any age can have problems with uroliths, but they are most common between the ages of 4 and 6 years. Male dogs have more trouble with uroliths than females because the longer, narrower male urethra tends to trap the stones.

Symptoms of Urolithiasis

The symptoms of urolithiasis are similar to those of cystitis. The dog may become incontinent or he may have difficulty urinating or experience discomfort toward the end of urination. A dog with urolithiasis may strain to urinate, especially a male with stones blocking the urethra. Urine may be tinged with blood. Complete blockage will cause cessation of urination, which, left untreated, soon leads to death.

Treatment and Aftercare

When the veterinarian examines a dog for urolithiasis, they will palpate the abdomen, take a urine sample, possibly X-ray the urinary system, and may insert a catheter up the urethra to locate the blockage. Some veterinarians will also perform an ultrasound exam of the dog's abdomen.

It's important that the doctor determine exactly which kind of uroliths the dog has. The various types are treated differently, depending on their mineral ingredients. Struvite or urate uroliths can be dissolved with a special diet or medication that affects the chemistry of the urine. Oxalate or cystine uroliths will not dissolve and must be surgically removed. Antibiotics are often prescribed to treat associated urinary tract infections.

Your veterinarian will instruct you on administering the prescribed medication and special diet for a dog with uroliths. The medication dissolves the uroliths the dog currently has, and the special diet helps prevent new stones from forming.

A dog who has had stones must always be allowed access to plenty of fresh drinking water. The dog's water intake and output must be sufficient to flush mineral crystals out of the bladder before they form into uroliths. It's very important that the dog also have opportunity to urinate as often as he needs. A dog forced to hold his urine for long periods is more likely to form stones, because the urine becomes overly concentrated.

Chronic Renal (Kidney) Failure

The kidneys remove toxins from the body. When they cannot perform this vital job, the dog becomes very ill. Left untreated, long-term kidney infections will eventually cause renal failure. Congenital defects and cancer may also cause the kidneys to fail. Renal failure is very serious and can cause death if intervention is not swift.

Any dog may be at risk for chronic renal failure, but symptoms generally do not appear until a dog is over 5 years old.

Symptoms of Chronic Renal Failure

When the kidneys fail, they become unable to concentrate liquid wastes, so an excessive volume of dilute urine is voided. To compensate for water loss, the dog may be very thirsty and drink more than usual. A dog in chronic renal failure will be generally ill and debilitated. He may vomit or have diarrhea, his breath will smell bad from his toxic internal condition, and he may have little appetite and may lose weight. The dog will appear depressed both physically and mentally.

Symptoms don't always show that a dog is experiencing this condition. A dog in chronic renal failure can appear normal until, suddenly, his kidneys shut down. This sends the dog into life-threatening acute renal failure.

Treatment and Aftercare

When a veterinarian diagnoses chronic renal failure, the dog will be placed on medication to correct his body chemistry imbalance and control the symptoms. The dog must also be fed a restricted or prescription diet to ease the load on his kidneys.

When the dog has recovered, he will still be fragile. He'll need to stay warm and well rested, and avoid any stress. You and your veterinarian will monitor your dog's progress by keeping close track of his weight. You may also be asked to record your dog's food and water intake and urine output.

A sudden change in your dog's behavior or activity level may be a sign of a health problem.

Endocrine (Hormonal) Disorders

The endocrine system uses the bloodstream to transport hormones. Hormones produced within the endocrine system affect the production and use of other hormones and body chemicals. Endocrine disorders can often cause elimination problems.

Cushing's Disease (Hyperadrenocorticism)

In a dog with Cushing's disease, the adrenal glands atop the kidneys produce too much cortisol (a form of cortisone). The most common cause is a pituitary brain tumor that secretes adrenocorticotropic hormone (ACTH) in large amounts. The ACTH stimulates the adrenals to overproduce cortisol. Another cause of Cushing's disease might be a tumor in the adrenal gland that causes it to secrete extra cortisol.

Cushing's disease can be genetic. Dogs who have been treated with corticosteroids are also at risk. These drugs are often prescribed for dogs with allergies and inflammatory conditions. This form is called iatrogenic (caused by medical treatment) Cushing's disease.

Increased thirst and increased urination are common signs of Cushing's disease. Increased hunger is another sign for many dogs. The excess water and food the dog takes in make him need to eliminate more often. Another symptom, muscular weakness, makes it difficult for the dog to hold his bladder and bowels. The dog will unavoidably break housetraining if he can't reach his potty area in time.

Other symptoms of Cushing's disease are symmetrical hair loss on both sides of the body, high blood pressure, thinning of the skin, fat deposits in the liver, calcium deposits in the skin, and plugged hair follicles on the belly. Many dogs diagnosed with Cushing's disease also have a history of recurring urinary tract infections.

Diagnosis can be difficult with this disease, sometimes requiring analysis of numerous blood samples.

Medication is the treatment most veterinarians choose for dogs with Cushing's disease. One medicine works by destroying part of the affected adrenal gland so it cannot produce such excessive levels of cortisol. A different medication, which inhibits steroid formation, is used for the pituitary-dependent form of Cushing's disease. Even when the cause of Cushing's disease is a tumor, most cases are not treated surgically because of the danger to the dog.

A dog diagnosed with Cushing's disease must remain on medication for the rest of his life to control this condition. The dog must frequently be retested to be certain he's still on the correct dosage as his body adapts to the medicine.

Addison's Disease (Hypoadrenocorticism)

Addison's disease is fairly rare, and most cases are the result of an atrophy of the adrenal gland. Addison's disease is the opposite condition from Cushing's. Cortisol production is deficient instead of overabundant. In Addison's disease, cortisol production is not the only problem, however, because other adrenal hormones also will be insufficient. Addison's disease can be fatal, because dogs can't survive without adrenal hormones.

Two iatrogenic forms of Addison's disease may occur in dogs with adrenal damage from having been overtreated with certain medications. One type is caused by overtreatment with corticosteroids for inflammatory conditions. Some of these patients recover after a while if the medicine is withdrawn, but in others the damage to the adrenal glands is permanent.

The other form of iatrogenic Addison's disease can occur in Cushing's disease patients who are overtreated with a drug used to control cortisol overproduction. In this form of Addison's, damage to the adrenal glands is permanent.

Depression is often the first symptom of Addison's disease. The dog may be weak, have little energy, and become anemic. Appetite may be diminished and the dog will lose weight from not eating enough. He may also vomit and have loose stools. Some dogs with Addison's disease drink and urinate a lot. An important clinical sign is that the symptoms tend to come and go.

Many of the illnesses that cause housetraining problems can be successfully treated with medication.

Diagnosis of Addison's disease involves blood tests to check levels of the chemicals produced by various organs. Because this disease is potentially life threatening, treatment may begin before test results confirm the diagnosis.

The patient is given replacements for the hormones he is unable to produce. Cortisone is the easiest to replace; low doses of the drug prednisone are used. The mineral-corticoids are more difficult to replace. These hormones normally regulate production of electrolytes, without which the body is unable to function. The medications for this can be given orally every day, injected monthly, or implanted under the skin in pellet form every ten months. A dog must be retested periodically to ensure proper dosage.

Diabetes Mellitus

Diabetes mellitus is a condition in which the dog has higher than normal blood glucose levels. Insulin produced by the pancreas normally controls the amount of glucose in the blood. With diabetes, either there is not enough insulin being produced or the body tissues do not respond properly to it.

Dogs at risk for developing diabetes are usually over 8 years old, although the disease has occasionally been diagnosed in pups under a year. Obese dogs are more likely to become diabetic. At highest risk are unspayed females.

Increased thirst and appetite are common early signs of diabetes. Even with an increase in appetite, however, there may be a loss of weight. Dogs with diabetes often have a poor coat. Cataracts can also be caused by diabetes.

A dog with diabetes will pass greater than normal quantities of urine because the bladder fills more quickly than normal. A dog cannot help urinating when his bladder reaches maximum capacity and the diabetic dog may have accidents at night or when he is shut inside without access to his elimination area.

Genetic Problems

Some elimination problems are caused by hereditary factors. There may be inherited structural or chemical abnormalities that lead to lack of control. Here are some common conditions that can cause elimination problems, and the breeds that are at greater genetic risk for them.

- Urolithiasis: Cocker Spaniel, Dachshund, Dalmatian, Miniature Poodle, Shih Tzu, Yorkshire Terrier
- Cushing's disease: Boston Terrier, Boxer, Dachshund, Poodle
- Diabetes mellitus: Cavalier King Charles Spaniel, Cocker Spaniel, Dachshund, Doberman Pinscher, German Shepherd Dog, Golden Retriever, Labrador Retriever, Pomeranian, Rottweiler, Samoyed

The best thing to do about hereditary problems is avoid them by getting dogs only from responsible and knowledgeable breeders. Reputable breeders test all their breeding stock for genetic conditions before mating them.

If you already have a dog with elimination problems stemming from genetic causes, follow your veterinarian's advice. Good medical treatment and home care can lessen the severity of many inherited problems and enable a dog to live a comfortable and happy life. Dogs with hereditary elimination problems should be neutered or otherwise prevented from breeding so they don't pass those undesirable traits to future generations.

When a dog first starts having accidents, owners may view the urination as a behavior problem and punish the dog or try harder to train him. This is useless, because the dog is sick and cannot help himself. If your housetrained adult dog suddenly begins peeing in the house at night or when left alone, take him to the veterinarian right away to check for a physical cause.

Advanced cases of diabetes exhibit alarming symptoms. The dog will act depressed, will breathe rapidly, and may vomit. An untreated diabetic dog will eventually stop passing urine. Shortly after that, he may go into a coma and die. Diabetes mellitus is nothing to fool around with. If you have any reason at all to suspect it, take your dog in to be checked. Left untreated, diabetes can kill.

When a veterinarian checks for diabetes, they will first give the dog a thorough physical examination that will include laboratory analysis of both blood and urine. The doctor may also X-ray the dog and/or do an ultrasound exam to look for structural abnormalities.

If high blood glucose levels are found, the veterinarian will start your dog on medications to help his body function more normally. The dog may need to be hospitalized for a few days to stabilize his condition. He will probably require daily insulin injections for the rest of his life to manage this disease. Your veterinarian will teach you how to medicate your dog.

Dietary modification is also important in the treatment and care of diabetes. If the dog is obese, his weight must be reduced. The veterinarian may place the dog on a prescription diet or recommend special foods. Stick with this regimen. Don't change the diet or give tidbits or treats unless the doctor specifically tells you it's permissible. Because a diabetic dog's blood sugar level depends on regular meals, you must be vigilant in keeping to the dog's feeding schedule. All dogs should be exercised daily and diabetic dogs are no exception. Exercise should be moderate, however. Strenuous bouts of activity must be avoided, as they could cause a sharp drop in blood sugar. With proper medication and care a dog with diabetes can live a comfortable and happy life.

Prostate Gland Disorders

The prostate gland surrounds the male's urethra at the neck of the bladder. If the gland becomes enlarged, it presses on the urethra and can cause urinary problems. The two conditions that most frequently cause this are prostatitis and prostate hyperplasia. Prostatitis is an inflammation of the prostate gland, generally caused by bacteria from the urinary system. This can be very painful for the dog. Prostate hyperplasia is not a painful condition, but it can cause urinary incontinence. Hyperplasia of the prostate occurs only in intact (unneutered) males. It most often shows up between the ages of 6 and 10 years.

Tumors, cysts, or abscesses of the prostate may also cause urinary problems. Neutering a male dog lowers his risk of developing prostate disorders.

Symptoms of Prostate Gland Disorders

Incontinence is a symptom of prostate disorders, and there may also be blood in the urine. Blood or pus may be passed from the dog's penis at times other than urination. The dog may strain to urinate or defecate. He may be constipated or pass ribbonlike feces.

Your dog relies on you to notice little changes that can signal big problems.

Treatment and Aftercare

The veterinarian will examine your dog thoroughly, including abdominal palpation, a rectal exam, and urethral catheterization to obtain samples for analysis. The vet may also use X-rays, ultrasound, or biopsy to diagnose the cause of the disorder.

If the problem is a tumor, cyst, or abscess, surgery will be done to remove the growth and probably the prostate gland itself. If the trouble is prostatitis, antibiotics will often take care of it, but castration may also be necessary. With hyperplasia, castration is often needed, although hormones or other medication may help.

Bowel Problems

Normally, the large intestine absorbs moisture from the feces before defecation. This way, the stool is well formed and excess water is not lost from the body. When anything causes the large intestine to absorb inadequate amounts of water, too much fluid will be excreted with the feces. The feces will be loose or watery, and bowel movements will be impossible for the dog to control. This is diarrhea, which is sometimes the reason for housetraining lapses. There are numerous causes of bowel problems, and the most common symptom of most of them is diarrhea.

If your dog has diarrhea, it's important to keep his backside clean. Carefully trim the hair around and below the anus so feces will not be caught there. If the dog's behind is very soiled, wash with water and mild dog shampoo and dry him thoroughly. If soiling is light, disposable baby wipes will do the job.

> ## Dehydration
>
> Diarrhea isn't just uncomfortable and messy, it can actually be very dangerous if it leads to dehydration. Dehydration results from excess water being lost through diarrhea, vomiting, or excessive urination. This can cause other body systems to malfunction. Dehydration causes a lowered blood volume, which can lead to fatal shock. If your dog has a very loose stool and/or is vomiting, watch carefully that he doesn't become dehydrated.
>
> An easy way to test for dehydration is to lift the skin on the back of the dog's neck, if it quickly and smoothly falls back into place, the dog is not dehydrated. If it remains pinched for a moment, it's likely the dog is dehydrated.

Chronic Liver Disease

The liver is an important organ for maintaining the health of the entire body. It produces blood proteins, converts waste products into substances the kidneys can excrete, processes and stores fats and carbohydrates, produces bile for digestion, and purifies the blood.

Older dogs are at risk for chronic liver disease, as are pups with congenital abnormalities of the organ. Common causes of liver disease are immune system or bile duct disorders, long-term inflammation, and cancer.

Symptoms of Chronic Liver Disease

Diarrhea is a common symptom of liver disease. Excessive thirst is another, and this may cause excessive urination. The dog may not want to eat and will lose weight. There may also be vomiting and abdominal swelling. A dog with liver disease will have very low energy.

Treatment and Aftercare

To diagnose liver disorders, the veterinarian will perform blood and urine tests, analyze abdominal fluid buildup, and may use X-rays or ultrasound. Sometimes the best way to determine the cause of liver problems is through biopsy or exploratory surgery.

There is no cure for chronic liver disease, but its progress can be slowed. The dog should be protected from stress as much as possible. He will need a special diet and plenty of rest. The veterinarian can prescribe medication to reduce fluid in the dog's abdomen and, possibly, antibiotics for specific cases.

Parasites

Parasites can cause chronic or acute problems with elimination. If your dog's bowel movements are very loose, tinged with blood, or have an especially foul odor, seek veterinary help.

Diagnosis of the specific parasite is necessary to prescribe proper treatment. Home remedies can be very dangerous. A favorite old-time "cure" for worms, tobacco, contains a potent nerve toxin that can miss the worms and badly sicken the dog. Over-the-counter remedies from the grocery or pet supply store are not always effective, and they can be dangerous if used improperly. Your veterinarian is the best person to decide which medicine will help your dog.

Worms

Worms that inhabit the intestines can cause bowel problems. Roundworms are common, especially in pups, and can cause diarrhea. Other common intestinal parasites that use canine hosts are hookworms, whipworms, and tapeworms. Some of these worms can afflict humans as well, especially children, so keep your dog free of worms for his sake and your family's.

If you suspect your dog might have worms, or if you just haven't had him checked recently, take a small fresh sample of his stool to the veterinary clinic. Your veterinarian can test for worms by examining a fecal sample through a microscope.

When giving your dog worm medicine, carefully follow your veterinarian's instructions or those on the product package. Your dog must be weighed to accurately calculate proper dosage. Weighing a large dog requires a platform scale, which your veterinarian probably has. A small dog can be weighed at home by holding him while you weigh yourself, then weigh yourself again

Parasites lurk everywhere outdoors and are easily passed on if your dog eliminates where other dogs with parasites have already gone.

without the dog and calculate the difference. Be sure to give only the dosage that's right for the dog's weight, because overmedicating with worming medicine can make a dog very ill.

Coccidia

Coccidia are microscopic parasites that rarely cause a problem unless the animal is under stress. Under these circumstances, the parasite can get a foothold and make a dog miserable with copious mucous-laden diarrhea. At risk for coccidial infection are nursing or recently weaned pups, dogs with a weak immune system, and those who have just moved to a new home. Because coccidiosis occurs with relative frequency in dogs soon after changing homes, this is considered a stress-related problem.

Dogs infected with coccidia are usually treated with sulfa drugs. Good sanitation of the home or kennel environment is vital to protect against the spread of the parasite. Coccidia oocysts (eggs) can survive for years and are resistant to most disinfectants. On hard surfaces ammonia compounds will kill the eggs, and steam cleaning can remove them from fabrics and carpets.

> ## Don't Hesitate to Call Your Veterinarian
>
> If your dog is slow to housetrain, has recurrent lapses in clean habits, or suddenly breaks elimination rules, be sure to check for physical causes. It does absolutely no good to scold or punish a dog for wetting or messing when he cannot control himself. In some cases, the stress of scolding can actually worsen the dog's condition.
>
> If you have any reason to suspect that physical problems might be affecting housetraining, take your dog to the veterinarian right away. Early treatment can cure or control most health problems that cause elimination troubles.

Giardia

Giardia are protozoan parasites that are acquired by drinking water from streams, ponds, and lakes that are contaminated with the microorganism. Giardia attack their host by attaching to the wall of the intestines. They reproduce there and are passed through the feces. It is not known if dogs and people can infect each other directly, but humans can contract giardia from the same water sources that dogs get it from.

Giardia is commonly found in dogs but doesn't always cause a problem. When it does, though, the dog will have diarrhea. The stools are soft, pale, and very foul smelling. Some dogs will lose weight and muscle condition.

Fecal examination is the method for diagnosing giardiasis. The most common type of fecal exam often won't turn up this pest, so a special technique is used. If your dog is diagnosed with giardiasis, the veterinarian will prescribe medication to eliminate the parasites.

Common disinfectants, such as chlorine bleach, can be used to kill giardia cysts in the dog's elimination area. Sanitation is important to avoid reinfection and to prevent the spread of the disease to other pets and family members. If your dog has been diagnosed with giardiasis and you have any similar symptoms, have your physician test you for the organism.

Viral Diseases

Distemper, parvovirus, and coronavirus can cause diarrhea, possibly with blood, and also vomiting, which can cause the patient to become dehydrated. A dog with any of these viral diseases will look and act very ill. Viral disease can quickly debilitate a young pup, but a high percentage can be saved if they receive prompt veterinary treatment. If you suspect your dog has a viral disease, call your veterinary clinic immediately.

At greatest risk for viral disease are young pups and elderly dogs. In those groups, the immune system is not always as strong as it needs to be to ward off viruses. In most cases, a properly vaccinated dog will be immune, but some may still contract a disease. Follow your veterinarian's recommended vaccination schedule.

Age-Related Problems

Some problems with elimination behavior have age-related physical causes. Training won't help these potty problems, but compassion and good care will.

Infancy

Infancy is the most common age-related cause of elimination problems. Luckily, this is cured by time, and a healthy pup will mature into a dog with good bladder and bowel control.

A young puppy's muscles and organs are not mature enough to completely control elimination. Also, a pup doesn't always understand or remember the housetraining rules at first. This combination of physical immaturity and social ignorance makes for some cleanup chores for you. Patience and consistency are the keys to housetraining. A good supply of paper towels will be helpful too.

A young puppy's muscles and organs are not mature enough to completely control elimination.

Until a pup is at least 4 months old, you should expect him to have elimination accidents. He's a baby and can't help it.

Senior Years

In his senior years, a dog may begin to lose strength in the muscles that control elimination. Age-related incontinence due to decreased muscle control may occur when the dog is awake or asleep. Never shame your old dog about this. He probably is already embarrassed that he can't control himself. Be patient and compassionate; your old buddy needs to know you care.

An older dog with incontinence should have a comfortable, washable bed. Synthetic fleece pads on top of absorbent washable or disposable materials will keep your dog out of his leaked urine. The bedding should be laundered as often as needed. The dog himself should be kept clean, too.

Learning More About Your Dog

Some Good Books

Health Care

Carlson, Delbert, DVM, and Liisa Carlson, MD, *Dog Owner's Home Veterinary Handbook,* 3rd edition, Howell Book House, 1999.

Fogle, Bruce, DVM, *First Aid for Dogs: What to Do When Emergencies Happen,* Penguin Books, 1997.

Pitcairn, Richard, and Susan Pitcairn, *Natural Health for Dogs,* Rodale Press, 1995.

Tellington-Jones, Linda, *Getting in TTouch with Your Dog,* Trafalgar Square Press, 2001.

Zink, Christine, *Dog Health and Nutrition for Dummies,* Wiley Publishing, 2001.

Behavior

Abrantes, Roger, Dog Language: *An Encyclopedia of Canine Behavior,* Dogwise Publishing, 2001.

Burch, Mary R., PhD, and Jon S. Bailey, PhD, *How Dogs Learn,* Howell Book House, 1999.

Fogle, Bruce, DVM, *The Dog's Mind: Understanding Your Dog's Behavior,* Howell Book House, 1992.

McConnell, Patricia, *The Other End of the Leash,* Ballantine Books, 2002.

Training

Alexander, Melissa, *Click for Joy,* Sunshine Books, 2003.

Aloff, Brenda, *Positive Reinforcement: Training Dogs in the Real World,* TFH, 2001.

Anderson, Teoti, *Your Outta Control Puppy,* TFH, 2003.

Benjamin, Carol Lea, *Surviving Your Dog's Adolescence: A Positive Training Program,* Howell Book House, 1993.

Cantrell, Krista, *Catch Your Dog Doing Something Right,* Lyons Press, 2004.

Jones, Deb, PhD, *Clicker Workbook: A Beginner's Guide,* Howln Moon Press, 1997.

Rutherford, Clarice, and Neil, David, *How to Raise a Puppy You Can Live with,* Alpine Publications, 2005.

Magazines

AKC Gazette
American Kennel Club
51 Madison Ave.
New York, NY 10010
www.akc.org

Dog Fancy
Fancy Publications
3 Burroughs
Irvine, CA 92690
www.dogfancy.com

Bloodlines Journal
United Kennel Club
100 E. Kilgore Rd.
Kalamazoo, MI 49001-5598
www.ukcdogs.com

Dog World
Fancy Publications
P.O. Box 6050
Mission Viejo
CA 92690-6050
www.dogworldmag.com

Videos

Rugaas, Turid, *Calming Signals: What Your Dog Tells You,* Hanalei Pets, P.O. Box 697, Carlsborg, WA 98324.

Carlson, Jeanne, *Good Puppy,* Sound Dog Productions, P.O. Box 27488, Seattle, WA 98125.

Dunbar, Ian, PhD, MRCVS, *SIRIUS Puppy Training,* James & Kenneth Publishers, 2140 Shattuck Ave. #2406, Berkeley, CA 94704.

Index

Photo Credits:

Kent Dannen: 1, 8–9, 34, 39, 41, 47, 48, 56, 57, 58, 59, 60, 67, 68, 69, 72, 77, 87, 91, 92, 94, 95, 99, 100, 106, 109, 111, 117

Jean M. Fogle: 4–5, 11, 13, 14, 17, 19, 20, 24, 25, 27, 29, 30, 32, 36, 37, 44–45, 46, 50, 53, 64, 65, 66, 71, 73, 76, 79, 80, 81, 84, 88–89, 90, 97, 101, 102, 114, 119